Collegial Teams

Collegial Teams

A Design for Improving School Performance

James E. Bruno
University of California
at Los Angeles

M.A. Nottingham
University of Southern
California

Lexington Books
D.C. Heath and Company
Lexington, Massachusetts
Toronto   London

Library of Congress Cataloging in Publication Data

Bruno, James E
    Collegial teams: a design for improving school performance.

    Includes index.
    1. Norwalk-La Mirada Unified School District. I. Nottingham,
M.A., joint author. II. Title.
LB2817.B75   379'.1535'0979493   75-10229
ISBN 0-669-08318-6

Copyright © 1976 by D.C. Heath and Company

Published simultaneously in Canada

Printed in the United States of America

International Standard Book Number: 0-669-08318-6

Library of Congress Catalog Card Number: 75-10229

Contents

List of Figures

List of Tables

Foreword

The Norwalk-La Mirada Unified School District is not unique as a setting for the pilot programs described in this book. Like many other districts, we face problems of declining enrollment (five schools have been closed), demands for improved student performance, and demands for greater teacher participation in district policy and decision-making procedures. We are funded considerably below the state average; yet, our citizens feel they are taxed to the limit for schools. The proportion of our student population needing extra help in learning basic skills is increasing.

From a very limited research and development fund, we have supported the collegial team internal shift analysis experiments for three years. Because of the results with students and the favorable reports from the teachers and administrators who have been involved, we are committed to continued support of the concept. I invite my colleagues in school administration to consider the facts reported in this book. I believe they will see the promise the concept holds for improving schools and that they will be interested in moving in that direction. I would encourage them to do so.

Maurice Ross, Ed.D., Superintendent
Norwalk-La Mirada Unified Schools
Norwalk, California

Preface

The plethora of educational innovations beseiging educational policymakers during the last decade has certainly made their jobs more difficult. Lawyers, judges, legislators, parents, and teachers are all demanding change in the hope of making our massive school systems more responsive to student needs. These innovations, some of which are not well evaluated for effectiveness, are thrust upon the schools with limited or unconfirmed results.

This book describes a unique experiment under way in a Southern California school district in which there is a precise functional division of labor between school administrators and teachers. Administrators set the goals and describe the payment for reaching the goal; teachers are given total professional authority to make all classroom decisions.

Teaching is getting more difficult. It is apparent that a larger effort on the part of teachers is required to maintain previous performance levels. This increased difficulty is most evident in urban school districts where the combined problems of children from advantaged backgrounds abandoning the schools in favor of private schools or fleeing to the suburbs, and the miniscule birth rate among those parents who could contribute the most toward forming positive educational attitudes are apparent. Zero population growth among the culturally advantaged classes and the still highly positive population growth rate among poorer economic classes has completely changed the makeup of most classrooms. The critical mass of poorly motivated students in many classrooms has been reached and effective instruction has come to a standstill.

Against this backdrop of declining enrollments and expending of higher teacher energy levels to maintain certain qualities, teachers have developed and endorsed a militant collective bargaining posture. Subjects such as curriculum decision making, teacher evaluation, and teacher financial compensation continually separate teachers from administrators and prevent them from effectively dealing with educational problems. Thus, in the future either the professionalism or collective bargaining model will be endorsed by the majority of teachers in school districts. Worsening working conditions resulting from the polarization of teachers and administrators in the collective bargaining process is the ultimate consequence of this process.

Teachers traditionally have not been provided with economic incentives to give proportionately greater attention to the slow learner or students who for some reason are considered difficult to teach. Failures in performance contracting were due primarily to the fact that the contractor could outperform the contractee in what the contractee could do, but did equally as poor in reaching students who are difficult to teach. Essentially, school districts wanted to pay only for those services that they found too costly or difficult to perform for themselves.

Merit pay, of course, has not been well received in educational circles for several reasons. Among them are its divisiveness, and teacher opposition. In addition, it does little to boost morale and unlike merit pay for piece work that is common in business and industry, the output in teaching depends upon the conscientious efforts of groups of people. The only sensible and viable type of merit pay for an organization where outputs cannot be traced to an individual teacher is group merit pay or school district profit sharing. Under this concept the entire organization is rewarded to the degree to which it meets is specified goals. Because different students require different marginal costs in terms of teacher inputs, the reward structure is based on the performance of the individual student, not groups of students, and the relative difficulty to teach that student.

To meet the threefold challenge of increased marginal costs of teaching (teaching becoming more difficult), trying to re-establish a "professional" type of teacher, and designing an incentive system that is not individual merit pay but group profit sharing, the collegial team concept was developed and implemented.

The purpose of this book is first to expose the reader, whom we assume to be school personnel, concerned parents, or graduate students in educational evaluation programs, to the collegial team concept and the compensation feature. Chapters 1 and 2 of the book, therefore, contain a background to the collegial team movement and the economic rationale for the compensation scheme, respectively.

Because the nature of any radical organizational restructuring of the educational delivery system requires excellent articulation of the concept and a time period for phasing in the program, immediate statistical types of empirical evaluation are inappropriate. Data, however, was collected at each of the school sites both on students and teachers. This data was analyzed and placed in such a form as to provide the reader with a capsule overview of what happened to teachers and students at each of the four school sites.

Chapter 3 reports the results of the collegial team concept in the cognitive growth area of reading. Comparisons of both intra- and interschool sites are given. Chapter 4 reports the results of an attitude survey given to teachers in which responses are geared to such dimensions of teacher behavior as curriculum decision making, teacher evaluation, professionalism, and so forth.

In addition to the limited empirical analysis presented in each chapter, a sophisticated longitudinal evaluation design is also provided. Bayesian analysis and stepwise multiple discriminant analysis procedures are outlined in the student and teacher effects chapters, respectively. Thus, these chapters should give the reader some insight as to the efficacy of the program and provide hints concerning how to perform an evaluation if implemented in a school district. The proposed longitudinal effects methodologies could also be incorporated as part of an overall evaluation of the collegial team concept in a school district.

The most important chapter in the text, from a school policy viewpoint, is Chapter 5 concerning the anecdotal and subjective evaluation that stems from the site principals and teachers. This chapter is also of critical importance for those contemplating the adoption of such an innovation in their own school district, since the anecdotal information provided by the principals provides the reader with useful insights into possible snags in implementation and outlines unforseen problems of the concept.

Appendix A contains a Fortran computer program with exemplary output to perform the net shift analysis, while Appendix B contains the actual attitude questionnaire given to the teachers at the individual school sites.

Finally, some words are in order concerning the appropriate use of the book by school policymakers interested in the possible adoption of the collegial team concept. First, no innovation can be transplanted per se from one district to another and be expected to enjoy successful implementation. Great care should be taken to make sure student, parent, and teacher groups are included in setting the design criteria for the compensation model. In addition, if in some districts, because of peculiar antagonistic relations between teachers and administrators, the concept can bring both groups together into meaningful discussions concerning how best to divide responsibilities to insure students are given the best possible educational program by the school district, then a positive result will have been gained. The collegial evaluation concept alone may become a major vehicle for professionalism in schools—by centering discussions around student needs and the best division of labor to satisfy these needs. Increasing professionalism in the schools is certainly a worthwhile goal if the schools are to meet the difficult challenges ahead.

Acknowledgments

The authors wish to acknowledge the support received from a variety of sources in their experimental work and in the preparation of this book. Major contributors to this effort have been the principals, teachers, and central office personnel in the Norwalk-La Mirada Unified School District, Norwalk, California. Superintendent Dr. Maury Ross, Assistant Superintendent, Dr. George Gustafson, and his staff have expressed a continuing interest in the collegial team concept and the incentive pay plan that provides some of the motivation for forming collegial teams. The fact that the district was willing to commit scarce research and development funds to the experiment over a three-year period attests to their innovative leadership as well as their commitment to the concept. Principals Don Henry, Jack Schirmer, Jack Hagthrop, and Howard Simons were particularly helpful in providing anecdotal records of collegial team behavior for the authors.

Additional support to the authors was provided by the Spencer Foundation through the Research and Publication Committee and Dean Steven Knezevich of the School of Education at the University of Southern California. This support was in the best tradition of the U.S.C. School of Education, which has compiled an enviable record in maintaining close working relationships with school districts throughout California.

Finally, the authors appreciate the efforts of numerous colleagues who have provided information, advice, and encouragement. In particular, Nancy Stricklin deserves commendation for her editing and typing of the manuscript.

Collegial Teams

1

The Collegial Team Concept

Introduction

The proper evaluation of teachers in the public schools of America remains an elusive goal. The system currently in operation in most schools, though often highly formalized in terms of rules and regulations, formal language, precise procedures, and closely monitored deadlines is basically ineffective in producing change or improvement.

This book is addressed to the problems of teacher evaluation, accountability, and incentives for improving performance. In it, the authors discuss the assumptions and realities of the current system and define the purposes of evaluation. A different set of assumptions and procedures designed ultimately to change the present system is a major theme of the book.

The content of the book is based upon the experiences of the authors in a variety of public school settings and upon empirical evidence acquired through a series of experiments conducted in elementary and junior high schools. The book was written to expose existing weaknesses in evaluation procedures, report the results of experiments using a different procedure with incentives, and to propose the expansion of that different procedure into all American schools. Such an ambitious and perhaps presumptuous goal must be approached boldly and rationally.

When the weaknesses of an existing system or procedures are critiqued, as is the case in this book, the critics have a responsibility to propose an alternative system. Essentially, the reader will find this book positive in that respect. The higher order view of human beings espoused by writers such as Maslow, MacGregor, Drucker, Likert, and Rogers lends support and strength to the authors' proposal. Schools in America are good. Few of us, however, would find them acceptable as they are. They can be improved, and they must be improved if society is to continue its support. The authors believe this book will contribute to that end.

1

The Context of Teacher Evaluation

The accountability movement that has characterized American education during the past decade is one manifestation of societal discontent with the performance outputs of schools. This discontent is especially focused on the student who is difficult to teach. Typically, he comes from a "disadvantaged" background, from a lower socio-economic background, from the culture of poverty. The Elementary and Secondary Education Act (ESEA) has concentrated resources from the federal government on the problems of educating children whom teachers find most difficult to teach. In the process, the teacher has been again singled out as the "critical point in the instructional delivery system." Thus in any discussion of schools and schooling, the concensus and needs of the teacher are critical.

The teacher does not operate in a vacuum without the influence of others in the school districts of America. His work is affected by a variety of individuals and public groups, all interested in the classroom process and its results. Among these is the local district board of education. This body, which represents the public at large, is at once the body most accessible in the democratic process and the embodiment of the public power structure. Its most important function is the selection of its executive officer, or superintendent. Together the board and superintendent are responsible for the policy decisions and executive functions designed to provide the most effective educational program possible within the resources at their disposal. Like teachers, their job is increasing in difficulty for a variety of reasons.

The board of education is the prime interface with the community it serves. Community is used advisedly here, because of the variety of value systems and concerns about schools that the board is forced to consider. Often the most critical within the community are the parents of children who were formerly left out of the instructional system because of the unique difficulties and extraordinary teaching effort required. More attention will be directed to these children as the incentive system that the writers propose unfolds. Significantly, as enrollment declines nationally, the numbers of students who were formerly left out—the potential dropouts and the children most difficult to teach—are increasing.

At the same time, and again because of enrollment decline, the teaching staff is getting older. For reasons that will be enlarged upon later in this chapter, this aging staff is not only more expensive, but more militant. This militancy is more organizational in nature than characteristic of the individual teacher. Teacher organizations, with whom the boards of education must deal, have not been particularly enamored with the accountability process, primarily because accountability processes make evaluation systems inevitable. Thus making teacher evaluation and accountability more effective and palatable becomes a major challenge for school policy makers.

One of the remarkable observations made by authors who have written about American education is the essential sameness they encountered in their visits to schools across the country (Silberman, 1970, pp. 121-22). The United States does not have a "system" of education in the sense that it may be found in such centralized regimes as South Korea or Sweden, and yet the variation in the many systems of education in the United States are differences in quantity of resources or physical arrangement but not differences in kind.

There are wide variations in sources of financial support for schools, both intrastate and interstate. There are some organizational differences including districts that are decentralized in their control mechanisms or organized horizontally rather than vertically. There are program variations too. Open schools, year-around schools, nongraded schools, self-contained classroom schools, and other configurations may be linked to individualized instruction, large group/small group instruction, and the use of aides and volunteers. The wide range of instructional material choices makes for additional variation in the learning environment a given student may encounter in a given school.

And yet the sameness is striking because the potential for variation is so vast. The sameness may be characterized by such factors as a principal for every school; compulsion in several forms such as in attendance or behavior norms (Silberman, 1971, p. 121); student-teacher ratios of limited variance; waiting, including waiting in lines and waiting for permission (Silberman, 1971); the single salary schedule for teachers; the emphasis on reading instruction in the early years of school; and the same kinds of people with the same philosophies and values operating in a bureaucratic model that is nearly everywhere the same.

The sameness of schools is not necessarily bad; sameness, per se, is neutral. It could be good or bad. In the context of this book, sameness provides a basis for being able to generalize. What is said about schools based upon a relatively small sample may be applicable to a much larger population. The authors believe the system for teacher evaluation fits that category, as does the increasing militance of teacher groups that is a concomitant.

In a few cases, evaluation procedures may be used to separate teachers from their profession, but the evidence suggests that this purpose is limited in value and is insignificant in numbers of teachers affected. In California, during an eighteen-month period beginning in 1971, for example, the California Teachers Association reported that a total of 63 teachers had charges leveled against them in which their competency was at issue along with a variety of other charges. Only 22 of those cases were heard. There were 16 dismissals (Action, 1975), or .0053 percent of a teacher population in California public schools that exceeds 300,000.

Teacher evaluation for promotion purposes is also limited, except to the degree such evaluation may assist the teacher in moving out of teaching into administration. But again, the declining enrollment problem means not only fewer teachers are *needed*, but also fewer administrators. In addition, there is a growing effort by teacher organizations to reduce administrator-to-teacher ratios. This movement, which has achieved some success, further limits the upward mobility of teachers. The result is an increasing frustration of the ego-status needs of ambitious teachers—a condition that can and should be ameliorated.

Tenure laws and the imprecision of the profession combine to make the dismissal of even the worst teacher subject to so rigorous a documentation process that the effort belies the result. The process is imprecise, frustrating, ineffective, and inefficient. A principal who decides a teacher is bad enough to warrant action for dismissal has saddled himself with the burden of proof, challenged an organization that is not devoid of its own power and influence, and condemned himself to hours of documentation in writing, only to have his own competence and integrity called into question by a hearing officer or a judge. It is not surprising that principals are reluctant to even try to remove a poor teacher. What is surprising is that the mechanics of the formal evaluation system include that expectation and then so nearly preclude its successful outcome. We think the principal has more productive uses for his time. If the formal evaluation system were to be viewed realistically in terms of its purposes and effectiveness, it could be placed in proper perspective and largely ignored.

And yet, Alexander Mood quoting Jacobsen in an HEW publication called *How Teachers Make a Difference* reiterated the problem with "ten percent of the teachers are excellent; ten percent are hopeless; eighty percent are the masses who are doing the job with varying degrees of competence and conscientiousness . . ." (Mood, 1971). It is not necessary to accept Jacobsen's figures to accept his point; not all our teachers are as good as we would like them to be.

One could say that the primary purpose of teacher evaluation is to improve performance. Improvement is a process of becoming better. It is evolutionary, and the need for it is never completely satisified (Glasman et al, 1974). So we evaluate to improve performance, or do we? A classic example may illustrate the problem.

The California legislature enacted a piece of legislation in 1971 called the Stull Act. It was hailed, at least by school administrators and legislators, as a tremendous addition to the accountability structure. It prescribed who was to be evaluated, by whom, when, and, by what criteria. Teachers were to be involved in the establishment of standards of classroom control, standards of the learning environment, and standards of student performance.

The reaction to the Stull Act was predictable. The initial flurry of activity and meetings resulted in formalizing and incorporating the provisions of the Act into the existing structure, so that although accountability as a process was given legislative endorsement, the system for evaluating teachers only increased in frequency and complexity, not effectiveness. The process became more formal, more proscribed by policy language negotiated by teacher groups, and less valuable in terms of improving performance.

In one school known to the authors, the Stull Act exposed the fact that some teachers had not been formally evaluated by an administrator for periods ranging from ten to eighteen years. After the shock waves abated and administrators had been properly reprimanded by higher administrators for their dereliction of duty (the higher administrators were joined by teacher organizations in deriding the poor administrative practices made evident), teachers were again evaluated routinely by the policy book—that is, by using a formal instrument devised by a representative committee of teachers and administrators. While administrators were asking other administrators why teachers had not been evaluated for so many years, one wonders why teachers did not *request* evaluation if the process was so important and valuable to them. There was no evidence that any teacher ever made such a request. Watching the whole incident unfold did little to inspire confidence in the teacher evaluation process.

Perhaps it is safe to conclude that the present system for evaluating teachers is ineffective, does not appeal to teachers or administrators, is based on the wrong assumptions, and is generally regarded as a waste of time by all parties to the act. Why are evaluation procedures with such a noble goal (improving performance) viewed with such distain or fear or both? Why is the system so formalized? Why doesn't it work?

The "Professional"

There is a great deal of talk about teaching as a profession and little doubt that teachers like to be regarded as professionals, but it is very difficult to be a professional in the public schools. There are at least three excellent reasons for that difficulty. One, the public schools are tax supported; that results in standards, policies, single salary schedules, and tenure. Two, the clientele of the public schools is mandated to attend; the professional has trouble selecting his clients. Three, the milieu in which the professional practices is a labor-management milieu; evaluation procedures put the principal in the "boss" role and the teacher in the employee role.

Probably little can or should be done about tax support for schools because that is society's method for transmitting its culture and values. Compulsory attendance also resists change if the purposes of schooling are to be served. But number three can be modified. There is a movement in the literature and the rhetoric, if not in fact, toward change in the administrator-teacher relationship based upon the "Y" theory management of MacGregor and the motivational hierarchy of Maslow. Involvement in decision making, participative management, decentralization and efforts to humanize schools as institutions are all positive concepts in the governance of schools. Changing the evaluation system seems a logical concomitant, as we intend to show.

The labor-management model for teacher evaluation may be the single most damaging ingredient in preventing the development of a profession in teaching. It contributes to the second-class status teachers are forced to acknowledge in salaries and clientele selection. The rigidity and formality of the process contributes to the ultimate in labor-management relations—that is, collective bargaining.

Collective bargaining for teachers, in those states in which it has become a legislative reality, promotes competing power structures. The board of education, superintendent, and other administrators represent the public power structure. The teachers' union establishes a competing structure that insists on negotiating wages, budgets, working conditions, class size, hours, and curriculum. In some school districts, the negotiations have threatened to tear the district apart: strikes, bitterness, jealousy, and hatred rend a people-intensive institution that can only work effectively in an atmosphere of trust. Trust means that people can depend upon each other to behave somewhat predictably. It also means that they can admit failure and ask for help. The labor-management model does not promote trust and negates professionalism.

To complicate further a situation that needs no further complication, administrators are forming organizations. Generally, they are middle-management groups—principals, primarily—who see themselves left out of the teachers' collective bargaining unit and therefore unrepresented in negotiations with the public power structure. The violence that this movement does to a management team concept is as yet unmeasured but is certainly cause for concern. How can a principal be the arm of the superintendent while he is at the same time building a parallel organization to negotiate directly with the board of education? Such a loyalty scheme is clearly anachronistic.

Teachers intuitively know the union movement is anachronistic for them too. Their loyalties are pulled in two directions; they want to be loyal to the public power structure, but they are dissatisfied with some kinds of administrative behavior and some of the meaningless processes they must endure. On the other hand, a recent survey of teachers in California confirms the lack of enthusiasm of teachers for collective bargaining. Collective bargaining ranked twenty-second on a list of activities they thought most important for their leadership to pursue (Action, 1975). Collective bargaining as a movement in public schools sharpens contrasts between groups working toward similar ends. Polarization tends to increase in a system that does not want polarization. Therefore, the contrasts are, to a degree, contrived.

As the struggle for power continues, we find teachers, as a subset of the school system, pulled by competing loyalties, and administrators, as a subset, deploring the collective bargaining movement while they organize to participate in it. At the same time, they, the administrators, contribute to collective bargaining for teachers by clinging to a formal evaluation system that does not work. In effect then, the schools, as systems, are moving *themselves* in a direction many of their members do not support.

A major contributing factor, aside from the organizational dilemmas already discussed, is the nature of teachers and their role perceptions. If teachers are ever to move toward more professional roles, they must change or be helped to change their perceptions of themselves. This point is perhaps best illustrated by Lortie (1971) in the quotation below:

It is not difficult today to find sweeping condemnations of the general level of performance among classroom teachers, condemnations whose grounds are rarely, in fact, made explicit or carefully documented. But one can be reasonably certain in asserting that teaching is not among those occupations where members play an active part in raising the general performance level of the field. Teachers are loath to hold each other to any set of explicit expectations for performance; classroom teachers, as a group, play little part in advancing the state of practice within their field. Whatever variations in performance may be within the occupations, we do not find a band of superior performers taking responsibility for upgrading general performance. A teacher may be considered outstanding by peers and public alike, for example, without showing interest in the performance capacity of teachers in general. The role, in short, is currently organized to exclude concern with systematic efforts to better standards or performance. In that respect, it is individualistic and, ultimately, conservative.

Lortie characterizes the work of teachers as individualistic and ultimately conservative. This means Teacher A has no responsibility for the performance of Teacher B. Many schools give the appearance of "cottage industries" when viewed from Lortie's perspective. Teacher A not only accepts no responsibility for Teacher B, but may actively resent B's excellence, if A views himself as less than excellent.

The authors contend that the less-than-professional concern displayed by teachers for the performance of their colleagues is a product of the system in which they work. There is no reward for professional behavior. There is little real expectation of it, or the expectation is unrealistic. The single salary schedule implies that all the teachers are equal, except in two rather unimportant dimensions—that is, years of experience and hours of college classes. For example, Teacher A, who is relatively new to the profession and knows that he is good, works next door to or in the same space with Teacher B. Teacher B is older, has been in the game longer, and is paid thousands of dollars more than Teacher A for a performance that both know is inferior to the work of Teacher A. That such a situation can exist may be best documented by examining the law that applies when the enrollment in a district drops. If fewer teachers are required than the previous year, the rule that applies is "last hired, first fired." Relative quality of teachers or an assessment of their performance levels is administratively and legislatively irrelevant. Examining formal evaluation forms is not a part of the process. As a result, since enrollment is declining nationally, teaching staffs are getting older. There is less new blood in the system, and perhaps less energy. Inherent conservatism has strengthened, and the system increases in rigidity. The formal evaluation system becomes more irrelevant as staff tenure approaches 100 percent.

The enrollment decline in American schools has other implications for teachers that are related to the evaluation procedures used and to their daily set of problems in creating a learning environment. The enrollment decline is not uniform. It tends to be more pronounced in affluent communities where the declining national birthrate is most evident. This subtle change results in a student population shift that tends to increase the percent of students from lower socioeconomic portions of the population. Children from lower socioeconomic backgrounds generally find it more difficult to learn in the public school system. Stated in terms of teacher effort, a larger proportion of students are more difficult to teach. As will be illustrated later, this factor becomes a major economic determiner of output effectiveness for teachers and is one of the prime reasons for forming collegial teams of teachers.

Discussions about managing schools must inevitably refer to the work of Maslow and McGregor. If we accept the human need hierarchy of Maslow, it is possible to link it to the "X" and "Y" theories of management proposed by Douglas McGregor. The fact is that McGregor and Maslow were colleagues at Brandeis University. McGregor has defined the "X" manager as one who believes that:

1. The average man is by nature indolent—he works as little possible.

2. He lacks ambition, dislikes responsibility, prefers to be led.
3. He is inherently self-centered, indifferent to organizational needs.
4. He is by nature resistant to change.
5. He is gullible, not very bright, the ready dupe of the charlatan and demagogue.

Most observers of schools would probably agree that as organizations, schools are operated as though the items above were a part of management's beliefs with the possible exception of number 5.

McGregor's (1957) theory "Y", in contrast, sees the role of management as:

1. Management is responsible for organizing the elements of productive enterprise—money, materials, equipment, people—in the interest of economic ends.
2. People are *not* by nature passive or resistant to organizational needs. They have become so as a result of experience in organizations.
3. The motivation, the potential for development, the capacity for assuming responsibility, the readiness to direct behavior toward organizational goals are all present in people. Management does not put them there. It is a responsibility of management to make it possible for people to recognize and develop these human characteristics for themselves.
4. The essential task of management is to arrange organizational conditions and methods of operation so that people can achieve their own goals *best* by directing *their own* efforts toward organizational objectives.*

Although the literature is heavy with discussions of participative management, shared decision-making and decentralization—which suggest that administrators and teachers see the need for changes in governance—the effects in terms of actual change are still minimal.

Collegial Teams

The linking of Maslow and McGregor allows us to consider a new set of assumptions about evalution in schools. We can begin to view teachers the way they want to be viewed—that is, as professionals. We could then admit the tremendous potential that exists in the staff of any school and design procedures for releasing that potential. What is needed then is a release mechanism that capitalizes upon Maslow's theory that people want and need to be self-actualizing. Self-actualization would seem to be an essential descriptor for a professional.

* Reprinted by permission of the publisher from *Management Review*, November 1957. © 1957 by the American Management Association, Inc.

The words "collegial team" as used in this context mean that people of similar experience and background are engaged in efforts to achieve similar ends. It implies that the efforts of members of the team can be mutually supportive and that the entire team can grow together as professional peers. It assumes a teacher can be self-induced to improve his teaching if the feedback he receives is worthwile in *his* eyes and if the feedback points out discrepancies by significant others (peers) (Glassman et al, 1974).

The assumption that a group of people who agree upon their goals and objectives can accomplish their ends is a reasonable assumption. Given the proper conditions and support, a collegial team can be relied upon to actively seek improved performance among themselves and thus improved results. They will become a self-actualizing group of professionals.

Collegial teams in schools should be formed voluntarily. The principal who expects that ideal will provide a set of conditions that encourages this to happen. He will ultimately insist that every teacher is a part of a collegial team. The first condition in promoting the formation of a collegial team is to understand the concept and the ingredients that will make it work. Both administrators and teachers need to thoroughly explore the concept. The principal who under-stands can help his staff understand so that resistance to change is reduced.

A collegial team has several functions, some of which are new to the members and some of which are extensions of functions they already perform. Initially, the functions of a collegial team can be expressed as four "P's": program, process, progress, and person-nel. *Program* means the team examines, selects, modifies, and implements the program of education in the school. *Process* means the team examines, critiques, evaluates, and suggests modifications in school processes. An example might be the attendance account-ing procedures. A collegial team could suggest ways to improve the process to make it more humane or more efficient. *Progress* means the collegial team evaluates how well students are doing. They determine the degree to which the objectives they have set are being achieved. *Personnel* means the collegial team selects its own mem-bers, accepts responsibility for their improvement, and evaluates the performance of members of the collegial team.

If interest in the formation of collegial teams is generated, then a more indepth analysis of its functions can be promoted. The remain-der of this chapter is devoted to that kind of analysis.

Functions of a Collegial Team

A collegial team of teachers in an elementary school could include the kindergarten through grade three teachers. A second team might include the upper grade teachers. The experimental work reported in subsequent chapters of this book was done with both configurations. The school principal is an ex officio member of all collegial teams in a school; his role is more explicitly defined later in this chapter.

Considering the rough division of functions outlined by the four "P's"—program, process, progress, and personnel—an analysis of each can begin. Program is defined as all the materials, objectives, and resource personnel for students immediately at hand at a school. A collegial team of teachers conducts a needs assessment of the community and the children for whom they are responsible. Their responsibility is to design a program that responds effectively to the needs of the students they serve. Generally, the teachers in a school, especially today's schools where the faculty is often very stable, can be extremely accurate in assessing student needs. They know historical performance levels, socioeconomic factors, parental expectations, and many other facts that can be used to clarify needs.

When needs have been clarified, objectives can be generated. A skilled principal can assist the team in developing objectives that are measurable, manageable, and nontrivial. Clarifying needs and objectives makes it possible to rationally select program materials. Program materials are available to assist a collegial team in reaching its objectives. Any teacher who uses them should be involved in their selection.

Other resources available should be enumerated by the collegial team. A reading resource teacher, for example, may become a part of the team and available to consult with the members who need extra support. In the process, that resource person may become unavailable as a substitute for absent teachers or as a vice principal, as is sometimes the case in schools now. In effect, the team clarifies the role of its members and of available resource people. Central office resource people may be explored for more effective contribution to the group effort at the same time. Too often in the present system, expensive central office resource people are underused at the local school level.

The program aspects of collegial team activity are not particularly new or startling; teachers have evaluated program components before. The deliberate fixing of responsibility for program development is nevertheless important to the potential for improving the performance of individual collegial team members.

Process evaluation is a legitimate function of a collegial team. Process evaluation means that any set of procedures in the school is subject to collegial team scrutiny. For example, a team might decide that the present conferencing process is counterproductive because students are not included; they could recommend to the principal that the process be changed. The team might also become more completely involved in structuring learning groups, time arrangements, schedules, discipline procedures, and attendance accounting. Once the functions of the collegial team have been defined and their responsibilities fixed, they, as a professional group, may recommend any process that research or their experience has demonstrated will facilitate attainment of the learning objectives they have developed.

Progress evaluation means the collegial team evaluates how well *they* are doing in reaching the objectives they have set for students. In Chapter 2, the interval shift analysis concept is explained as a method for involvement of the collegial team, the administration, and other resources in establishing the parameters of the system and measuring the results. Collegial team evaluation of outputs is broader than standardized testing but does not eliminate that useful method of providing group data. In the thrust for individualization, many other kinds of data are collected by the team to monitor progress and measure results.

The final "P"—personnel—is the evaluation area that is the most difficult to achieve and yet the most vital if teachers are to break the labor-management cycle and enter the professional world. It represents a major break from tradition and requires more than lip service by administrators to the "Y" theory management concepts of McGregor, the participative management practices of Drucker (1968), the qualities of Likert's (1967) concept of an "E" leader, and the higher order view of Maslow's self-actualizing man.

Collegial team evaluation of personnel means that teachers accept some responsibilities for their mutual growth. The process releases potential. The formal, restrictive, labor-management model is replaced by an open atmosphere of trust and the free exchange of useful information and positive criticism. How can a team of teachers be convinced that mutual evaluation is productive? How can fear and distrust be dispelled? What procedures will promote meaningful evaluation related directly to the major purpose of improving performance?

Personnel Evaluation in a Collegial Team

Collegial team evaluation rests upon several well-documented assumptions. These are:

1. The labor-management evaluation model is counterproductive in terms of improving teacher performance.
2. Maslow's view of human needs applies to teachers, too. Teachers want to behave more professionally than the traditional system allows or promotes.
3. Teacher judgment is at least as good, and probably better, especially in a group setting, than the judgment of a single administrator.
4. Peer pressure for improvement is more effective than administrative exhortation or fear-producing evaluation instruments.
5. Better teachers in a collegial team can exert positive influence upon poorer performing teachers.
6. Traditional evaluation procedures that attempt to separate teachers from the profession are more trouble than the results obtained justify.
7. Principals can acquire the necessary human relation skills, management skills, and learning theory to effectively promote a collegial, professional, productive, and creative learning environment for children.
8. Teachers and principals are not equal in ability, commitment, or energy.

Beginning with assumption eight, we suggest that the evaluation system used by a collegial team must be individualized in the same sense that learning for children is individualized. A collegial team acquires from the literature or develops for itself a variety of data collection instruments for use by its members. These evaluation data sources run the gamut from subjective sources to very objective sources. Classroom visitation is only one of many possible evaluation data sources. It has, of course, been traditionally the only evaluation data source used by administrators unless we count the grapevine, student comments, and other informal sources.

A variety of evaluation data sources from which collegial team members can choose is necessary because teachers are different. Our objective is to make the selection of sources voluntary so that the trust level will rise and the threat threshold can diminish. We might illustrate the point with the diagram shown in figure l-l. S and I represent two extremes of a spectrum of teachers. S teachers are most secure. They know they are good teachers. Teachers near the I end of the spectrum are more insecure, less effective, and easily threatened by formal evaluation procedures. Teacher A in the diagram is more effective and secure than Teachers B, C, D, or E. Teacher E is the least effective and most insecure member of the team. One of the major goals of the collegial team concept is to move teachers on the spectrum in the direction of the arrow. Secure, effective teachers will exert positive professional influence on teachers who are less secure if the collegial team concept is developed. Experimental findings supporting this assertion are presented in later chapters of this book.

Earlier it was stated that teachers join a collegial team voluntarily, at least in the initial stage of development. If a vacancy occurs on the team, the team conducts interviews to fill that vacancy. The principal, as an ex officio member of all collegial teams in a school, may participate; he may even reserve the final decision for himself if trust levels are not as high as they can be. The team selection process helps commit the team to the welfare and improvement of its members. No one wants to be a loser, and no one wants a decision he helped make to be wrong. The collegial team can be relied upon to assist new members in the effort to accomplish the objectives of the team. Generally, a new team member will be selected because he brings particular strengths to the team that the team has decided it needs.

The variety of evaluation data sources a collegial team needs may be categorized into at least three areas. These are (1) self evaluation, (2) peer evaluation, and (3) student evaluation. From a variety of evaluation data sources, each team member selects one or more that would be least threatening for him. As the team gains in sophistication and mutual trust, its members can be encouraged to increase the number, variety, and comprehensiveness of the evalua-

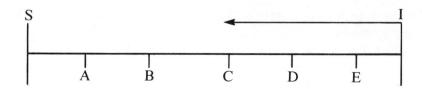

Figure 1-1. Increasing Positive Teacher Attitudes through Collegial
Teams.

tion data sources they choose. The team soon learns that evaluation
data sources are not *against* the teacher but *for* the teacher. In the
process, the least secure member is encouraged to move toward the
most secure member who is willing to use many evaluation data
sources.

A key factor in collegial team evaluation is that each member
agrees to share the results of the evaluation data sources he chooses
with the team as a whole. Self-evaluation in such a setting can be
most rewarding, particularly if the self-evaluation takes the form of a
video tape record of a teaching performance. Other less threatening
self-evaluation data sources that might be selected include self-
administered rating scales and check lists, examples of which may
be found in Miller (1972) and Glasman et al. (1974).

Peer evaluation can include a wide variety of evaluation data
sources and is ultimately the most all-encompassing and productive
category when the data collected is shared as a whole. Peer evaluation can also include the round table process where the team thinks
together of ways to help each of its members improve. Among the
instruments that can be included in peer evaluation are:

1. *Peer rating scales,* which are most effective when combined with
   direct experience with the teacher being rated. Observations in a
   variety of school settings including the classroom, form the basis
   for completing peer rating scales. As indicated earlier, such
   scales, some well-validated, are available from several sources
   including Miller and Glasman et al.
2. *Lesson analysis* is a form of peer evaluation that focuses attention on sharpening teaching techniques. It may involve a single
   teaching episode or become a routine practice among the members of a collegial team. Recall that a teacher being critiqued
   selects this option, if it is used at all.

3. *Class assignment analysis* is an option that might shed light on teaching skill, the teacher's concept of the importance of the curriculum area involved and his view of students. Sample assignments might be exchanged on a regular basis with a set of criteria developed by the team as a guide to the critique of assignments.

4. A *critique of objectives* could become a valuable peer evaluation technique. The whole accountability process becomes increasingly effective if teams of teachers avoid duplication of effort and jointly prepare objectives that are comprehensive, meaningful, and measurable. Not everyone writes good objectives, but everyone could contribute thoughtfully to the development of objectives of significance. The anxiety that accompanies administrative efforts toward accountability might thus be effectively reduced.

Objectives are at the heart of planning curriculum and strategies for structuring learning. A collegial team should be involved in their development, in the procedures for monitoring progress toward them, and in their final outcome measures.

Student evaluation of teachers as an optional data source probably has limited utility in the elementary school. At the college level, student evaluation is regarded as a highly reliable tool (Glasman et al, 1974). In the upper elementary grades, however, simple attitude indicators for student response can be administered. The increase in student alienation from school with increased age does suggest that some effort should be made to discover why more and more students like school less and less as they get older. Such evaluation data sources might be most valuable if designed and administered as a collegial team activity rather than as an evaluation tool for individual teachers.

Implementing Team Evaluation

Implementing a collegial team evaluation scheme requires planning, understanding, and commitment. The following conditions would appear to be minimal if success is expected:

1. The whole purpose of forming a collegial team would need explanation and understanding.

2. Teachers would not be forced into collegial teams but would be encouraged to organize for this purpose voluntarily. The experi-

mental work of the authors, reported in later chapters, suggests that at least in the experimental setting used, the resistance to forming a team is minimal.

3. The principal would agree to accept the evaluations of members of the collegial team regardless of the specific evaluation data sources they individually chose.

4. All team members would agree to participate in team evaluation by using at least one individual evaluation data source plus whatever "hard" data the team agreed to gather as a whole group in compliance with school board regulations or state law.

5. As an ex officio member of the collegial team, the principal is free to question procedures and evaluation data sources, but he must agree to sign the official evaluation form for each teacher on the team (since the team has already been involved in producing it, and he trusts their judgment) and forward it to the central office for filing or whatever is required by the formal evaluation policy.

6. The collegial team is not restricted to self-evaluation, but it is encouraged to evaluate processes, programs, progress, and even the principal as a group of responsible professionals.

7. The collegial team is encouraged to modify existing models or generate their own evaluation data sources.

8. The collegial team decides the uses to which funds from an experimental incentive system, such as that described in succeeding chapters of this book, will be put, including the option of paying themselves an incentive salary.

Role of the Principal

Most authorities agree that the role of the principal is absolutely crucial to the successful operation of a school. The authors contend that his two most vital functions are (1) improvement of curriculum and instruction, and (2) personnel development. Forming collegial teams with teachers will promote both these functions.

In a "Y" theory school, power is distributed because power is a function of knowledge, and the principal does not have a corner on the market. Authority rests in offices, therefore the principal has authority. The principal shares his authority but does not abdicate his responsibility. Participative management does not mean lack of leadership nor irresponsibility by the principal.

Earlier, we assumed that the principal has, or could acquire, the human relations skills, learning theory, and management skills necessary to contribute to the professionalism of his staff. In that role, the principal is a questioner. He questions plans, instruments, programs, processes, and personnel. He is a problem identifier. He knows success is not the absence of problems but their definition and resolution. He does not avoid problems or cover them with jargon. He separates them from mere symptoms and involves his professional teams in their resolution or amelioration.

The principal is a facilitator. He helps collegial teams accomplish their objectives. He listens to their concerns. He consults with them. Sometimes he objects, especially if their plans are too ambitious or too selfish or when he is sure that what he knows about how children learn is being violated.

Finally, the principal is a decision maker. In crisis situations, he is the final authority in the school. In other matters, he is a communicator seeking information before making decisions. He is a skilled leader.

In the early history of schools in the United States, there was no principal. It was only after schools grew from one room to multiple rooms, many more students, and thus more teachers, that teachers decided they needed a "principal-teacher." That teacher was a facilitator of a collegial team. As public schools expanded, differentiation became more pronounced. As school organizations became more complex, the functional specialization inherent in Weber's bureaucratic model completed a separation of administration from teaching that resulted in the formal line and staff arrangement common in school organization today.

It may be useful to remember the principal-teacher or head-teacher concept prevalent in early American education because that model has relevance for the collegial team concept advocated here. In this context, we can repeat three earlier paragraphs *almost* verbatim.

It may be assumed that *teachers* have, or could acquire, the human relations skills, learning theory, and management skills necessary to contribute to their own professionalism. In that role, the teacher is a questioner. He questions plans, instruments, programs, processes and personnel. He is a problem identifier. He knows success is not the absence of problems but their definition and resolution. He does not avoid problems or cover them with jargon. He separates them from mere symptoms and becomes involved with his colleagues in their resolution or amelioration.

The *teacher* is a facilitator. He helps his students accomplish their objectives. He listens to their concerns. He consults with them. Sometimes he objects, especially if their plans are too ambitious or too selfish or when he is sure that what he knows about how students learn is being violated.

Finally, the *teacher* is a decision maker. In crisis situations, he is the final authority in the classroom. In other matters he is a communicator seeking information before making decisions. He is a skilled leader.

We intend to show here that the relationship among teachers and between teachers and the principal is historically and logically that of a professional team. The necessary functional specialization inherent in a large school organization need not be allowed to destroy that team relationship. The fact that a destructive relationship is currently going on, or in place in schools, does not mean that it must continue. We contend that the ubiquitous labor-management model for the evaluation of teachers is the key organizational element driving the school system to collective bargaining. Collective bargaining appears to result in the removal of control of the schools from their public ownership and place that control in the hands of union negotiators. We doubt seriously that such an arrangement will be in the best interests of students or teachers; we think that teachers prefer to be professionals and that this arrangement is in concert with public expectations.

Since the labor-management model for teacher evaluation is a major contributor to the collective bargaining movement, we propose that the model be changed. As succeeding chapters report, we believe that the collegial team approach to evaluation provides a set of conditions that help teachers move toward the professional status they desire. Further, we believe that the best interests of students will be better served by teams of professional colleagues coordinated and facilitated by administrators than by the adversary relationship collective bargaining produces.

Summary

In this chapter, we have briefly explored the context in which teachers perform in schools today. We have pointed out the discrepancies in the labor-management evaluation model for teachers and the forces within the school system that are moving it in a direction its members do not want to go. The problems associated with declining enrollment and near l00 percent tenure among teachers, together with the proportional increase in the number of students considered more difficult to teach, have been defined.

The desire of teachers to be regarded as professionals has been contrasted with the forces that inhibit movement in that direction with major emphasis on the labor-management model for evaluation. Finally, we have introduced a different evaluation model for teachers, which we call the collegial team. The collegial team has been defined and a conceptual framework for its development and implementation has been described.

In succeeding chapters the collegial team concept will be linked to an incentive system that is based upon concepts from micro-economic theory and is related to the labor-intensive system found in public schools. Evidence and data obtained from this initial experiment will, it is hoped, set the stage for a major change in the way teachers view themselves and their role in the public schools. In the process, new ways to deal effectively with the major issues of the l970s, namely, professionalism versus collective bargaining, teacher evaluation, and providing for effective treatment of a student body considered increasingly difficult to teach will be presented. A $60 billion enterprise in which local budgets are typically 85 percent committed to personnel costs certainly deserves the attention it gets from the public, from legislators, and from its critics, both inside and outside the system. The fact that the system remains at least somewhat open to change provides a positive setting for continued efforts to release the potential that inevitably exists in America's most noble institution, the public schools.

2

A Model Incentive System for Elementary Education

Problems of Change in Educational Organizations

It is extremely difficult and sometimes even counterproductive to discuss alternative criteria for designing incentive systems in education. How does an organization, as political and labor intensive as education, with its strong teacher unions protected by tenure-type personnel systems, develop the required flexibility to deal with issues and crises that society demands be resolved in the schools? As discussed in Chapter 1, of primary consideration is an incentive system which insures and enhances the professionalism of teachers. This professionalism can only be maintained and strengthened by teachers themselves performing the necessary evaluative tasks designated by society. The model incentive system proposed here, unlike previous attempts in this area, is not dependent upon individual merit, but is similar to *group* legal, engineering, and medical practices. The group in this case is the collegial team which incorporates a hierarchy of teaching professionals involved with the instructional process.

It was no accident that education was not organized with the collegial team approach and that educators found themselves locked in the fixed-step salary schedule. In previous decades, educational performance was not of such overriding societal concern, and there was a healthy symbiotic relationship between administrators and teachers. Thus, there was no need for the type of functional specialization and differential reward system required by modern educational practice. Today, with parents demanding that fair instructional attention be given their children; with performance dropping, as measured on standardized tests; and with administrators finding themselves unable to deal decisively and effectively with teacher competence (as mentioned in Chapter 1) a solution within the organization itself must be sought, and, more importantly, teachers must themselves assume the largest role in solving the primary problem of teacher evaluation. This latter requirement is especially critical for an effective incentive system because of the rapid growth of collective bargaining and teacher unions in American education.

In order to influence organizations to change and adapt to new societal demands, careful attention must be directed at how the incentive criteria are designed to affect change. In elementary schools, there are at least four groups who are intimately concerned and affected by any changes in organization. The peculiar needs of these groups must be, therefore, considered foremost if the innovation is to take hold and not be another in a long list of educational innovations to achieve its Hawthorne effect and then be summarily dropped as the important parties lose interest.

Participants in the Model

The first and most important consideration in the elementary school incentive model is the student, or the recipient of the instructional process.

Students

Students vary tremendously in abilities and learning styles. Present compensation schemes provide little incentive for teachers who work with students considered difficult to teach. Rewards, if they are given at all, are typically a simple linear function of the number of students progressing, or they are based upon changes in group averages. Thus, in these incentive systems, high-achieving students tend to counteract the poor performance of the less able. Student progress must, therefore, be scrutinized as far as student-teacher interaction is concerned, and any financial incentives in the elementary school should be weighted heavily toward those students most difficult to teach.

In recent years, increasing student performance has, especially on standardized tests in mathematics and reading, been one of the central objectives of many school districts. In fact, this single output of schooling formed the basis for the accountability movement in education during the late 1960s. The performance-based contracting concept is an excellent illustration of how the educational establishment responded to this demand. Outside contractors (private firms) subcontracted with the schools to teach basic skills for a fee. They, in turn, guaranteed student performance on these tests. Compensation for the contractor was typically based upon a fee for each student moved one grade equivalent of growth in some cognitive area.

Performance contracts were written between teachers and school districts as in Mesa, Arizona (Filogamo, 1970) and school districts with private corporations such as in Texarkana (Hall, 1970). For an excellent summary of why these radical educational experiments failed, see Hall and Stucker (1971). This reference also contains a total evaluation of the concept at sites throughout the country where the experiment was conducted. Performance contracting failed essentially because its performance was not any better than that of the schools themselves especially with the poorer, more difficult to teach student.

In all the experiments, traditional statistical evaluation methods were used to determine the amount of compensation and to evaluate program success. Traditional statistical types of analysis, such as analysis of variance, t-test, analysis of covariance, and so forth, were found to be inappropriate for compensation of performance contractors since they typically concerned themselves with changes in mean scores and thus tended to mask what changes were occurring in other intervals of the frequency distribution. For example, a student gaining .2 grade equivalent in a cognitive area totally balances two children losing .1 grade equivalent growth. Yet, it might be more important for the school district to know that two students fell behind than to know one student gained in a given elementary school. At best, these standard statistical techniques give a static, dichotomous (significant/not significant improvement) assessment of the achievement gain. The concern over changes within the distribution was pointed out in an excellent paper by Lindman (1970) in research conducted for the Center for the Study of Evaluation.

Based upon past experience, a performance-based compensation scheme must recognize four important premises:

1. Individual students learn at different rates.
2. The costs to the contractee or teachers in the incentive system are composed of fixed costs that are independent of the level of output and variable costs that are positively related to level of

output. Moreover, teacher variable costs are constant per unit of input—that is, the hourly rate for a teacher is constant no matter how many hours of teaching are required.

3. The contractee or teacher is a profit maximizer (e.g., he will not work beyond the point where costs exceed income).

4. The school district desires to reach a certain specified output at minimum cost and place financial incentives in those areas that are costly to the district and difficult to achieve. In essence, the contractor is a utility maximizer.

From the above premises, certain theorems emerge concerning the design of an incentive system. These are:

1. From 1 and 2, we find that different costs will be associated with teaching different students the same amount.

2. From 3, we can stipulate that the contractee or teacher in the incentive system will not operate beyond that point where revenues associated with producing one more unit are equal to the costs associated with producing that unit of output. (In economic jargon, this principle says that the profit maximizer produces only to that point where his marginal revenue equals his marginal cost.)

3. From 4, the school district would like to target those sectors of the student achievement distribution that it finds most costly or most difficult to achieve and would therefore desire to place rewards in the system in an effort to maximize its own utility.

The last two points will be discussed in greater detail later in the chapter.

Unfortunately, most performance contracts between schools and the private sector placed the school districts somewhat at a disadvantage, since they usually contained only two simple objectives: increase the achievement of each student by a given amount—Specified Change—or increase achievement above a specified norm—Specified Norm (Fox, 1970).

In the case where a contract stipulates a set amount to be paid for each student who improves a given amount (an example of this type of contract is in operation in the Texarkana school district where, in 1970, the Dorsett Company received $80 for each student who improved one grade level on independently administered standardized achievement tests within 80 hours of instruction) and assuming the profit maximizer has techniques to separate the faster from the slower learners, the financial incentive will be to focus upon the faster learners in order to assure at least a partial payoff. Secondly, the fast learners are less costly to teach than the slow learners (since, under our assumptions, costs are related to the time required to teach a stipulated amount), thus the contractee will maximize his profits by educating the fastest learners first and then proceeding to the slower ones until his time constraint is exhausted. Finally, the profit maximizer will not undertake the teaching of any student who will cost him more to teach than he will receive in revenues. (For public relations purposes, he might make a token gesture.) The profit maximizer might take some financial loss on a few students during a small experimental trial with the hope of winning a larger contract at some later date. In the long run, however, it is in the best interest of the profit maximizer, in this type of contractual setting, to concentrate his efforts on the faster learners at the expense of the slower ones. Thus, a performance contract that pays a specified amount for a specified change will yield incentives that will favor faster learners over slower learners. Moreover, it is likely that few resources will be channeled into teaching the slower learners. In a specified change type of contract, therefore, rewards are not given to those changes the school district finds most costly and difficult to achieve by itself.

Under the specified norm type of performance contract, the contractee is compensated according to the number of students he raises above a specified norm. This type of contract was operative in the Banneker School in Banneker, Michigan where Behavioral Research Laboratories received in 1971 $800 per student per year, which was the same amount spent for conventional instruction. In this program, an independent evaluator tests students after three years, and $2,400 is refunded for each child not at national achievement levels or above. This type of contract contains all the pitfalls of the specified change contract. In addition, we see that different students must be moved different amounts. Ceteris paribus, those students further below the norm will be more costly to bring above the norm than those students closer to the norm. Moreover, there is an incentive to raise the student just far enough above the norm to virtually guarantee that he will still be above the norm at the time of testing. Under this type of contract, we would expect to see a grouping of students just above the national norm and another grouping of students far below the norm.

In economic terms, the critical issues concerning incentives in incentive systems center about the fact that the contractee or teacher faces a constant marginal revenue schedule—that is, he is rewarded equally for each student educated—while he faces an upward sloping marginal cost curve (assuming he educates the least costly students first). One method of dealing with this problem of decreasing incentive is to design the incentive system so that the rewards or marginal revenues increase with the number of students reaching a set goal. Figure 2-1, which is discussed in a later section on the economic basis for the model incentive plan, illustrates an increasing marginal revenue curve. Such a reward curve would give additional incentive for the performance contractor to focus on slow learners.

It is obvious that students form the first and most essential part of the design for an incentive system. The technical details of the model elementary school incentive system as related to students will be discussed later in the chapter. A second design criterion, to be considered next, is the promotion of greater autonomy of teachers over instructional decisions, which would thus result in an increase in teacher professionalism.

Teachers

Most opposition to incentive schemes from organized teacher groups revolves around the point that determining individual merit causes problems in morale in the organization and invariably leads to comparison of teachers (rate busters). The isolation of teachers that results from merit pay and the failure to reward all the support functions that are required in an instructional delivery system are also cited negatively. Present merit schemes, by definition, are dysfunctional in combining teaching talents toward achieving a set goal. They tend to create minimal concern for the teaching performance of colleagues and retard the sharing of experiences and effective teaching techniques. They strengthen the isolation of teachers and reinforce the lack of responsibility for colleagues' performances, as discussed in Chapter 1. Thus, *team* approaches to teaching and functional specialization are discouraged rather than encouraged under present payment schemes.

The nature of teaching is such that increased professionalism— where teachers are given decision-making authority and responsibility in the instructional process—is the key to increased performance of teachers. Divisive schemes that do little to instill a colleague relationship can only be counterproductive to an organization in which effectiveness is almost totally based upon cooperation and mutual assistance for success at the elementary school level. Finally, everything in the instructional process is so interrelated that one really cannot evaluate teachers in isolation from the school climate and from the influence of colleagues.

The established system, organized along set classroom units, promotes the notion of integration, coordination, and organization on paper, but few teachers know what is going on in other classrooms. The effectiveness of teachers in the fourth grade depends upon what was accomplished by the third grade teachers. Yet, there is very little formal interchange of ideas, identification of common problems, and sharing of effective teaching strategies among these teachers.

Team teaching, when practiced correctly (not where each teacher does his or her own thing), is the first step toward achieving professionalism among teachers. The *collegial team* approach moves even further in this direction because it includes (1) a multitude of classroom units (not one), (2) has an incentive system designed to insure that performance outputs are met (not just payment according to the fixed-step salary schedule), and (3) increases the professional responsibility and authority of each team member to include such tasks as the performance evaluation of other teachers and a direct voice in the purchase and use of instructional materials.

The most important aspect of professionalism among teachers—the evaluation of each other's professional competence—is not promoted with current educational practices. Instead, as mentioned in Chapter 1, administrators have been expected to evaluate teachers. The process, however, is ineffectual, partly because the teachers rarely, if ever, get unsatisfactory ratings, and partly because the administrators may not be the most competent personnel in the organization to perform the evaluation. In addition, administrative evaluation of teachers tends to move teachers into a collective force for resistance.

Teachers are in the best position to evaluate other teachers, and more importantly, they are more likely to get cooperation from poorer teachers toward increased performance, since they are not placed in the adversary teacher-administrator role. Thus, since teachers are given the responsibility for instructional outputs, they should have a greater voice in how the process itself is organized, how the instructional needs of each individual student can be met, and how evidence can be gathered for various forms of evaluation.

The next element to be considered within the framework of the proposed model includes the personnel in the school district who provide the instructional support services available to the teaching staff.

Supervisors and Specialists

Those who organize, facilitate, coordinate, and supervise the instructional delivery system are typically not included in incentive schemes. While many teachers will report favorably upon principals, curriculum supervisors, and audio visual specialists and their value to improving instruction, their current utilization in districts is probably quite low, even though millions of dollars are poured annually into instructional support services. Because of lack of incentive, only a few teachers avail themselves of these services.

This low utilization of instructional support services occurs because these personnel are not attached to classroom units or to specific children, nor are they evaluated toward the performance of a set goal. School districts typically utilize these personnel only when especially called by a teacher or group of teachers to perform some service. The model incentive system, in which these support personnel are made to feel a part of the educational process, can only help improve their performance.

Teachers, singly and in separate classrooms, often have difficulty in "asking the right questions," whereas groups of teachers aware of problems involving a group of classrooms, or even a school site, might identify and isolate specific educational problems where these instructional support resources can be put to good use. For example, children with cultural diversity from all classrooms could be given extra attention in areas of basic skills. Instructional packages and self-programmed materials could also be designed (since economies of scale would lower the cost) for remedial work in specific subject matter areas. With large numbers of classrooms involved in the incentive system, economies of scale allow these instructional support services to be both efficient and effective.

Finally, in this section on the participants in the model incentive plan, we deal with the person most often neglected in designing incentive systems—the school administrator.

School Administrators

The school administrator typically receives a higher salary than teachers (although the per diem gap is narrowing significantly), not because he is the "best"teacher, but because he supposedly has managerial and personal skills that allow him to lead an organization. Yet, administrators seem to find themselves performing tasks that could best be done by teachers, while teachers, on the other hand, often feel that administrators are overpaid, since they know teachers could perform such tasks and many believe they could perform them much better. Evaluating teaching is one example. Ideally, the school administrator would prefer to have a plan that provides teachers with financial incentives toward increasing student performance while at the same time inhibiting the divisive nature of schemes based upon individual merit. He would also like to see improved results from the effective use of the huge investment the school district has made in instructional support. For a manager of the educational enterprise, a kind of school district profit sharing is more realistic than individual merit. Peer pressure to perform from colleagues, as discussed in Chapter 1, might achieve desired results more efficiently than the administrative pressures that are typically used.

The administrator's role in the design of an incentive system is, therefore, most important. He is involved in setting the goal upon which incentives will be based. In the model incentive scheme, the administrator, working with teacher groups and central school officials, determines the performance objectives for achieving system-wide goals. These objectives can be related to cognitive output in the elementary school, as in reading or mathematics, or the objectives can be related to affective student behavior, such as attendance and dropout prevention at the secondary level, or a combination of both is possible. The key notion is that the administrator provides the resources that are required to achieve the agreed-upon performance objectives; teachers, on the other hand, are given full professional decision-making power in implementing the means for achieving their performance goals.

In Chapter 1, the collegial team approach was presented as the means for realizing improved educational performance. Thus far in this chapter, the participants considered in the design of a model incentive scheme that effectively utilizes the team concept have been discussed. The next sections of this chapter present a specific design for an incentive-based plan employing the collegial team approach. The design criterion for this school district "profit-sharing" incentive scheme will be placed upon only the cognitive output area, although the methodology is generalizable to other school performance and output areas.

Theoretical Economic Basis

Principles of marginal analysis in microeconomic theory form the basic rationale for the design of the model elementary school incentive pay scheme. In a straightforward piecewise merit or incentive plan, the teacher would receive compensation for each student reaching the target distribution. Such a system is depicted by a linear marginal revenue curve as shown in Figure 2-1. If 50 percent of the students reach a certain performance goal or objective, the teacher receives 50 percent of the reward or incentive.

Unfortunately, the degree of difficulty for reaching a performance goal such as a grade equivalent of growth is far from equal across students as the linear marginal revenue curve assumes. Some students, by virtue of their home backgrounds, native abilities, and other factors, will improve in performance with little or no teacher effort. Some students will demand an inordinate amount of teacher effort to reach the goal. The marginal cost curve to achieve the goal, in terms of teacher and school district resources, is highly nonlinear.

Theoretically it is in the teacher's best economic interest to teach students only up to the point where the MC (marginal cost) curve intersects the MR (marginal revenue) curve. Efforts beyond this point cost the teacher more than he receives. The crucial component of the design is to closely approximate the MC curve with an exponential MR curve so that greater incentives are placed on those students who were formerly left out without penalizing those who normally achieve well. Figure 2-2 illustrates this concept. The exact

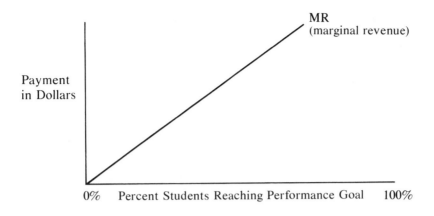

Figure 2-1. Marginal Revenue Curve.

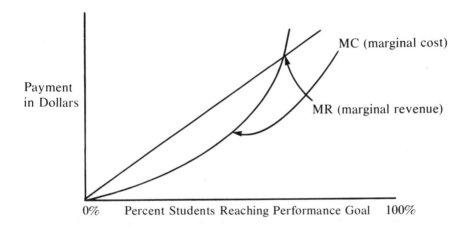

Figure 2-2. Marginal Revenue-Marginal Cost Curves.

shape of the exponential curve is determined by agreement among participating teachers, members of the support system, and the school administration.

In view of the breakdown of parental controls and the radical changes in the composition of school population that has resulted from a heavy influx of low socioeconomic-status students, the point of intersection of the marginal revenue-marginal cost curve is actually declining or moving further to the left. It is definitely getting more difficult to teach or, stated differently, to maintain last year's performance; more teacher cost is required. Unless incentive systems recognize this fact, we should see rapid and cumulative deterioration of performance. Increasing marginal cost of teaching is extremely important for districts to consider. Inflation further complicates the picture because higher levels of resource allocation will be required to maintain constant performance, and those levels may themselves be inadequate.

To derive the incentive payment schedule, the following tasks must be accomplished by school officials:

1. The level of aggregation of students has to be agreed upon (class or grade or school or district).

2. All personnel having input to the instructional process at the agreed-upon grade levels must be identified (teachers, supervisors, specialists, coordinators, aides, and so forth). The goal here is to place incentives toward functional specialization and to assist weaker members of the team rather than to promote morale-weakening entrepreneuring. Instructional materials and other school district resources should be better utilized under such a scheme.

3. The target or goal distribution for the program must be identified. For example, one goal might be that at the end of the year each student must be achieving at a specified grade level; other examples are that each student must achieve one grade level of growth or that each student must achieve his projected growth as determined by some expectancy formula.

4. Parameters of the model must be defined either by negotiation or by empirical research. These parameters are (a) the total bonus available, (b) how the reward will be divided (equally or percentage of salary or as a lump sum to the team for their choice of uses), (c) total amount available in the supplementary plan, if desired, to reward those who go beyond the goal, and (d) the minimum percentage of students who must reach the target distribution before qualifying for the supplementary plan. The shape of the exponential payment plan or marginal cost curve is determined by agreeing on payment for 50 percent achievement of the goal. It is this latter parameter, which reflects the MR-MC curve, that is most critical to this scheme.

Once the above issues are resolved, the model incentive payment plan is relatively easy to implement.

Compensation Properties

To understand the payment schedule for the proposed incentive pay scheme, consider the curves depicted in Figure 2-3. Notice the shape of the curves is determined by specifying the payment the district would make to the instructional team if 50 percent of the students achieved the desired goal. This point should be mutually agreed upon by the instructional personnel involved and school officials. Possibly last year's standard or percent of students reaching the goal could be used as a starting point in negotiations. Different schools in the district might have different MR curves.

In Figure 2-3, points A, B, C, and D refer to the amount of compensation the team is to receive if one-half the students under their charge reach the desired goal. The general formulas for the curves are based upon the exponential function: $Y = ce^{ax}$, where in curves 1 and 2, $a > 0$; in curve 3, $a = 0$; and in curve 4, $a < 0$. Notice that: a controls the shape of the curve; c equals the total bonus or compensation available for distribution ($1,000); x is the percent of students reaching goal; and y is the total payment to the team. If the 50 percent point is exactly half the total bonus, the exponential function is a straight line: $Y = cx$.

Curves 1 and 2 are most appropriate (where a is greater than 0) since they weight payments for performance toward reaching those students who are most difficult to teach. Curve 3, which illustrates a straight line payment schedule, most closely reflects the current single salary schedule payment procedure. Curve 4 is shown here merely to illustrate the way in which the curve is affected by a change in the value of a. Curve 4 would result in greater incentive pay for students who are easiest to teach, a condition that would not address the problem created by the increasing numbers of students who are more difficult to teach.

Under this formula, for example, if the agreed-upon compensation curve were to be designed so that 50 percent ($X = 50\%$) of the students reaching the goal (one grade equivalent of growth) would result in a payment of $250 ($Y = 250$) from a total payment potential of $1,000 ($C = 1000$), then the exponent for the payment curve a would equal two ($a = 2$).

Thus, a very realistic approximation of the actual marginal cost curve at a particular school site can be characterized by these exponential functions (see Tables 2-1 through 2-3 for a series of

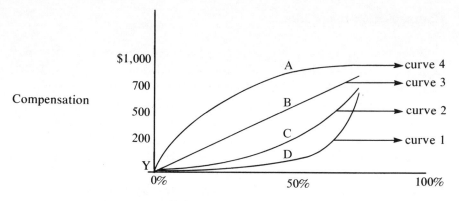

% of Performance Goal Met such as Percentage Students Gaining 1 G.E.

Figure 2-3. Alternative Incentive Pay Curves.

Table 2-1
Payment Schedule: Figure 2-3, Curve 1
Midpoint at $300
Total at $1000

Percent Achieving Goal	Payment for Teachers
0.04	3.73
0.08	12.44
0.12	25.15
0.16	41.46
0.20	61.08
0.24	83.84
0.28	109.58
0.32	138.19
0.36	169.56
0.40	203.61
0.44	240.26
0.48	279.46
0.52	321.15
0.56	365.27
0.60	411.77
0.64	460.62
0.68	511.77
0.72	565.18
0.76	620.84
0.80	678.69
0.84	738.71
0.88	800.88
0.92	865.17
0.96	931.55
1.00	1000.00

Table 2-2
Payment Schedule: Figure 2-3, Curve 3
Midpoint at $500
Total at $1000

Percent achieving goal	Payment for Teachers
0.04	40.00
0.08	80.00
0.12	120.00
0.16	160.00
0.20	200.00
0.24	240.00
0.28	280.00
0.32	320.00
0.36	360.00
0.40	400.00
0.44	440.00
0.48	480.00
0.52	520.00
0.56	560.00
0.60	600.00
0.64	640.00
0.68	680.00
0.72	720.00
0.76	760.00
0.80	800.00
0.84	840.00
0.88	880.00
0.92	920.00
0.96	960.00
1.00	1000.00

payment schedules based upon varying exponential functions).
Again, empirical research at a particular school site could be used to
determine the exact shape of the curve for that school and thus the
payment schedule that would result. It is expected that this important parameter would, in practice, be determined in a collegial
atmosphere of mutual concern. Of course depending upon socioeconomic characteristics at each site one might derive different
marginal revenue curves.

Exemplary Analysis

The following data was used in the preliminary design for the
Norwalk-La Mirada Unified School District. In this district it was
observed that the reading scores at School A in the district were not
adequate and needed to be improved. The single salary schedule did

Table 2-3
Payment Schedule: Figure 2-3, Curve 4
Midpoint at $700
Total at $1000

Percent Reaching goal	Payment for Teachers
0.04	190.83
0.08	272.62
0.12	335.87
0.16	389.46
0.20	436.85
0.24	479.81
0.28	519.42
0.32	556.37
0.36	591.13
0.40	624.06
0.44	655.43
0.48	685.45
0.52	714.27
0.56	742.03
0.60	768.85
0.64	794.81
0.68	820.00
0.72	844.47
0.76	868.30
0.80	891.52
0.84	914.19
0.88	936.34
0.92	958.00
0.96	979.21
1.00	1000.00

not provide the incentive for improved performance on the part of the teachers. The goal distribution and parameters for the model were established as follows:

1. Of the students in grades 1, 2, and 3 at School A, 90 percent will individually show a minimum of ten months' gain for the school year as measured by the Cooperative Primary Reading Test.
2. The incentive bonus for teaching personnel will be $1,000, with $500 in the extra bonus plan. The 50 percent point will result in a $250 payment and the exponential function will be: $y = ce^{2x}$ or $y = 1000\ e^{2x}$, where c = total payment = 1000 and x = % reaching target distribution.

The extra bonus is designed to reward the instructional team not only for reaching the desired minimum goal (90 percent of all students gaining ten months of growth) but for achieving higher growth levels among some students. These additional growth levels are summed for all students, and teachers are paid in a linear fashion for the total growth above the desired goal; ($y = bz$) where b is the weight given the total growth of students beyond the established goal, and z is the cumulative sum of the gains that exceed the target. For the Norwalk-La Mirada Unified School District, the value of b was set equal to $25 so the formula was $y' = 25z$. If 90 percent of the students in grades 1, 2, and 3 reached their targeted growth and a cumulative 10.0 grade equivalents of extra growth was achieved for all students, then a total of $250 in addition to the amount paid for 90 percent of the students reaching the goal would be paid by the district to the collegial team. In effect, the collegial team gained an additional $25 per grade equivalent for each student or combination of students who exceeded the target growth of one grade equivalent. This procedure ensures that collegial team attention will be directed to students who are easy to teach as well as those who find learning more difficult. The payment schedule, based upon this particular MR curve, is shown in Table 2-4. For the supplementary bonus, the teachers are compensated according to the formula: $y' = 25z$, where z is the cumulative additional performance. A computer program written by the authors (see Appendix A) performed the required analysis. The illustrative outputs shown in the first example below were based upon the data in Table 2-5 and thus use only the difference between pre- and posttest scores. (Note that both examples below illustrate the computations needed by the model.)

Example 1 from Table 2-5 illustrates a situation where all students achieved at least one grade level of growth. Therefore, the teachers qualify for a supplementary or an additional bonus.

Example 1 (Minimum growth required–1.0 grade equivalents; Percent reaching goal–1.00; Grade–2):

The percentage reaching the goal $= 1.00$;

The incentive bonus for the teacher, regular plan $= \$1,000.00$;

The bonus for the teacher, supplementary plan $= 30 \, [b = 25$ and $z = 1.2$, where $y = (25) (1.2) = 30$ (students 4 and 5, Table 2-5)];

The total incentive bonus for teachers $= \$1,030.00$.

Based upon the data presented in Table 2-6, Example 2 illustrates a situation where most, but not all, students achieved one grade level of growth. The 90 percent target was not achieved for the group as a whole.

Table 2-4
Payment Schedule: Figure 2-3, Curve 2

Percent Achieving Goal	Payment for Teachers
0.10	10.00
0.20	40.00
0.30	90.00
0.40	160.00
0.50	250.00
0.60	360.00
0.70	540.00
0.80	640.00
0.90	810.00
1.00	1000.00

Table 2-5
Illustration 1: All Students Achieve at Least One Grade Level of Growth

Student I.D.	Entry Score	Post Score	Diff. Pre-Post
1.	2.00	3.00	1.00
2.	2.00	3.00	1.00
3.	2.00	3.00	1.00
4.	1.00	2.50	1.50
5.	1.00	2.70	1.70

Note: z = (cumulative additional performance) 1.2 attained by students identified by numbers 4 and 5.

Example 2 (Minimum growth required–1.0; Percent reaching goal–.75; Grade–2):

The percent reaching the goal = .75;

The incentive bonus for the teacher, regular plan = $510.00;

The bonus for the teacher, supplementary plan = 0;

The total incentive bonus for teachers = $510.00.

The model incentive pay scheme demonstrated in the above examples can be easily modified to deal with performance objectives for attendance and dropout rate reduction. Empirical studies would be necessary in order to establish the marginal cost curves for achieving each objective. Experience criteria would then provide a marginal cost curve that comes closest in approximation to reality.

Table 2-6
Illustration 2: Less than 90% of Students Achieve One Grade Level of Growth

Student I.D.	Entry Score	Post Score	Diff. Pre-Post
1.	1.50	2.50	1.00
2.	1.50	2.50	1.00
3.	1.70	2.50	0.80
4.	1.00	2.90	1.90

The parameters for the model can be renegotiated if the initial curve proves to be significantly out of phase with actual school experience.

Some Additional Notes on the Model

The incentives a collegial team receives for working with students are paid at the end of the year when student performance results are known. When the amount has been determined, the team is notified of the amount. The collegial team decides, as a unit, how they want the incentive pay to be used. They may decide, as has been the authors' observation to date, to use the funds for the purchase of additional materials for program support. They may decide, however, to pay themselves on a pro-rata basis or upon any basis they desire. The point is that the incentive funds are put at the disposal of the collegial team. Ultimately, incentive pay schedules could be set by local boards of education in a financial plan designed to substantially reward teams of teachers on the basis of improved student performance.

In the experimental work of the authors, students were not considered in the analysis if they missed more than 20 percent of the days of possible attendance, either through transfer or absence. Thus, the compensation plan is "fair" in that it only evaluates the performance of students with whom teachers have been able to have reasonable instructional access.

The supplementary incentive plan is to reward teachers who go beyond expectations with bright students, while at the same time not penalizing the underachieving students. Before teachers qualify for the additional compensation plan, 90 percent—or some other agreed-upon minimum percentage—of the entire target group must have achieved the performance goal.

Summary

In summary, there is presently a need in education for designing a logical and consistent method for merging teacher compensation schemes with student performance. The design proposed in this study is based upon a modification of Bruno's (1972a) "Interval Shift Analysis" and incorporates two additional key features. First, the incentive is placed with the instructional team (teachers, specialists, administrators, aides) for improved organization of instruction. Second, increased financial incentives are provided for teaching students who are more difficult to teach. This latter objective is satisfied by deriving the financial payment scheme from a nonlinear or exponential curve rather than a linear curve. Payment is then based upon a percent of students reaching a certain target distribution or goal. A supplementary bonus plan for the instructional team is then available for teaching excellence beyond this minimum performance goal.

The procedure described in this chapter is intended to provide a useful supplement to compensation of teachers on the fixed step salary schedule and, hence, can be considered a form of merit pay. The notion of merit, however, is transferred from individual teachers to instructional teams. This tends to encourage more colleague interaction, functional specialization, and it develops collegial pressure to encourage poorer teachers to improve their performance. The organization of the instructional system is given to the teachers and support personnel rather than being the sole responsibility of administrators.

As previously mentioned, the nonlinear payment schedule is designed to give greater instructional attention to the formerly "left-out" students in the classroom and establishes true merit. The supplementary bonus plan is used to encourage overall excellence in teaching all students, regardless of ability.

The inherent limitations of the fixed-step salary schedule, which places financial incentives on years of experience and numbers of graduate units, both of which have proved to be minimally related to pupil performance, have provided the need for incentive payment plans. With birth rates declining, particularly among high socioeconomic groups, and the amount of new teacher talent diminishing, many school districts are faced with mounting problems that derive from teacher aging, tenure, and poor performance. A new, properly designed incentive pay scheme is needed to encourage improved performance by teachers. Incentive pay schemes, based upon designs similar to the one presented here, can be effectively used to improve the school district instructional program. For example, by increasing the levels of aggregation from the group of grades 1, 2, 3 and 4, 5, 6 used in this study, to whole schools and even school districts, interesting possibilities for developing instructional performance based incentives schemes in school finance plans might be devised. Certainly societal demands for accountability on the part of teachers and school districts will tend to accelerate efforts toward some form of incentive pay, and teachers groups would seem to prefer this kind of school district "profit sharing" for involved groups of teachers rather than merit pay for individual teachers.

The next chapters focus on the empirical research conducted to determine the impact of the collegial team on both students (Chapter 3) and teachers (Chapter 4). More importantly, however, research designs and methodologies for assessing the long-range impact of collegial teams are proposed. The reader is especially directed to these sections, since they elucidate how the collegial team concept can be evaluated for effectiveness in school districts that might consider utilizing the concept.

3

Evaluating Cognitive Growth of Students

Most educational innovations are evaluated principally along the dimension of their influence upon the cognitive growth of students. The educational accountability movement in education, as well as the concern of judges, lawyers, legislators and parents, will tend to insure that educational innovations continue to be measured against standards in the cognitive growth area. While the use of educational vouchers and performance contracting attempted to increase school productivity (again, when measured with the criterion of cognitive outputs), the collegial team concept directs attention to the fact that in many school systems administrators are faced with low productivity of teachers who are older, have tenure, and are becoming closer in attitudes to the collective bargaining militant posture rather than the professional posture characteristic of teachers in previous years. With the decline of enrollments and absence of new teaching talent, well-designed incentive programs based on the collegial team concept can meet the three challenges to education in the future; namely, the rise of teacher militancy, increased difficulty of teaching (as classes become dominated by students from poorer socioeconomic backgrounds), and increased demands for teacher accountability.

Of course the collegial team concept can be evaluated with criterion-referenced testing measures as well as norm-referenced tests. Criterion-referenced tests can be used as an output of the collegial team concept if, for each grade, the set of tasks, skills, knowledge, and so forth are defined and the degree to which each grade meets these criteria are defined.

Preliminary Analysis

In previous chapters, the basic theory of the collegial team approach and the internal shift analysis method of team compensation were presented. This chapter directs attention to the actual experimental work conducted in the Norwalk-La Mirada School District. Preliminary findings are reported for three elementary school sites and one

45

intermediate school site in the area of changes in student cognitive growth. The parameters for the compensation model[a] as defined in Chapter 2 were (1) each student was expected to achieve one grade equivalent of growth in reading; (2) if 90 percent of the students achieved this growth, then the collegial team would receive additional compensation at the rate of $25.00 for each additional cumulative grade equivalent of growth achieved; and (3) the total incentive for each school site was $2,000 for 100 percent achievement of the goal and $500.00 for 50 percent achievement of the goal. Students missing more than 20 percent of the instructional days available during the year were not considered in the plan, nor were newly arrived transfer students.

The preliminary analysis is broken down by school site in the following subsections to provide the reader with a more comprehensive view of the instructional environments in which this educational innovation took place. In order to provide meaningful comparisons of cognitive growth, the collegial teams at each school site were compared against regular classrooms within their own school and other schools in the district that were judged by school officials to be comparable for purposes of control. Because of differences in leadership styles of the principals, articulation of the concept, and small sample size (number of sites), the findings presented below should be considered only as preliminary in attesting to the efficacy of the collegial team concept. The design for a more comprehensive long-range evaluation of the collegial team concept and its import upon cognitive growth is presented later in the chapter. Readers planning to utilize collegial teams in their school districts should pay particular attention to this concluding section.

School Site A

School Site A is located in a predominantly white middle-class neighborhood and at the time of the experiment possessed a student body with an average IQ of 105. The typical track record in reading achievement for this school was approximately 30 percent of the children reaching one grade equivalent of growth each year. Students at the third-grade level were reading 3.0, 3.8, and 3.7 in years

[a]Note the parameters for the compensation model were revised by teachers and school officials for 1974-75. A $2000 total bonus with a $500 bonus for achieving 50% of the goal were specified. Ninety percent minimum cutoff was used to qualify for additional funding.

1971, 1972, and 1973, respectively. Thus, the average grade-level norm seems to indicate the school performance was average, if, of course, expected performance at the end of grade three is considered acceptable at 3.8 for the group as a whole.

The leadership of the principal at this school site can best be described as very good, with the principal himself supporting the innovation enthusiastically. Unfortunately, there was a large turnover in staff during this period; thus, a great deal of inservice training had to be given, and difficulties in the implementation of the program and articulation of the team concept consequently developed.

The school site in the district most closely resembling Site A—and thus used as a control for the project—in terms of ability of students and racial composition had approximately 280 students at grades 4-5-6 with typically only 100 reaching one grade equivalent in growth each year.

At School Site A, 260 students were involved in the experiment in grades 4, 5, and 6. The average reading pre- and posttest scores for grade 4 were 4.2 and 5.3; for grade 5, the average pretest score was 5.4 and post was 6.4; for grade 6, the pretest score was 6.6 and post was 7.3. Based upon the analysis, 48.6 percent of the students involved in the program achieved the required grade equivalent growth of 1.0. The rest of the school site achieved approximately at its average of 30 percent. This team, while not qualifying for additional or supplementary funding, nonetheless received $488.48 under the basic collegial team plan. One grade equivalent or higher was gained by 128 students, while some gained as much as 2.3 grade equivalents.

In summary, the program was judged successful at this site although the full potential of the concept was not exploited because of the large staff turnover. In terms of cognitive growth, the program did outperform the comparison school and those grades not part of the collegial team within the school.

School Site B

School Site B is a predominantly white middle-class school with a history of average achievement. In the third grade, reading scores for 1971, 1972, and 1973 were 3.3, 3.7, and 3.7, respectively. The average IQ for this school was approximately 110, and historically, only 45 percent of the students had gained one grade equivalent of growth each year.

The leadership provided by the principal at this school site was excellent and was described by school officials in such terms as energetic, innovative, and very supportive of the project. Staff relations were excellent, and in the inservice programs given, the rules and guidelines for implementation of the project were closely followed.

The most comparable control school was also the school used as a control to Site A. Similar student backgrounds, as well as faculty characteristics, restricted the comparative analysis to this school where only 100 out of 180 students reached one grade equivalent growth in reading.

At School Site B, 203 students in grades 4, 5, and 6 were involved in the experiment. The average reading scores, pre- and posttest, were 3.9 and 5.3 for grade 4; 5.5 and 6.9 for grade 5; and 6.3 and 7.0 for grade 6. Of the total of 203 students involved in the experiment, 126, or 55.7 percent, reached one grade equivalent of growth in reading. The bonus allocated for this site was, therefore, $619.72. The largest individual gain in reading was 3.8 grade equivalents. School B performed in an exemplary manner under the collegial team concept and was judged successful when compared with the control school. The excellent leadership provided by the principal probably contributed to the growth exhibited by all children in the school; hence, the advantage of the collegial team per se in terms of cognitive growth was not as dramatic. Although it should be noted that most of the poorer ability students at the school were receiving instructions by the collegial team.

School Site C

School Site C experimented with the collegial team concept at the lower elementary level, or grades 1, 2, and 3. While this school site had the largest Mexican-American student population of any school site used in the experiment, it has historically been one of the best performing schools in the district. In a typical year, 50 percent of the students reach one grade equivalent of growth. The average IQ for students at this site was 112. The average third-grade reading scores for the years 1971, 1972, and 1973 were 3.4, 3.7, and 4.1, respectively.

At this site the principal was described by central administrators as seeking opportunities to promote his school. Staff leadership was relatively high and staff relations were described as better than average. The closest comparison school had 140 students in grades 1-2-3, of which only 70 reached one grade equivalent of growth.

At Site C, 161 students participated in the experiment. The average pre- and posttest scores for grade 3 were 3.2 and 4.0; for grade 2, 2.4 and 3.4; and finally for grade 1, 1.0 and 2.1. In grade 1, a pretest was not given, but all students were assumed to start at the 1.0 level in reading. Of the 161 students, 80 reached one grade equivalent growth or better, with the individual high being a growth of 3.8 grade equivalents. Since 51.0 percent of the students reached the goal in reading growth, the bonus for this collegial team was $510.00. The gains exhibited by this school contrast markedly with the comparison school in which only 29 percent reached one grade equivalent of growth.

School Site D

Finally, Site D was a collegial team experiment performed in a junior high or intermediate school setting. Site D can be considered one of the best performing schools in the district, with typically 50 percent of the students reaching one grade equivalent of growth each year. The average IQ at this school site was 105. In 1972, 1973, and 1974, the eighth-grade reading scores were 6.5, 7.5, and 8.1, respectively. This school site also has a significant number—132 out of 818—of Spanish surname students.

The principal at this experimental school was described as easygoing, nondirective, and supportive of the project staff. The school was considered a relatively easy assignment for the staff since it is in a more affluent area of the district. The closest comparison school had 200 students in grades 7-8 with 100 reaching one grade equivalent growth in reading.

At Site D, 676 students participated in the experiment and the average pre- and posttest scores for reading in grade 7 were 6.5 and 7.4. For grade 8, they were 7.7 and 8.5. Of the 676 students, 284, or 42 percent, reached the goal. The bonus earned was then $353.00.

In summary, the schools used in the experiment have been relatively stable in ethnic composition during the time period under consideration; hence, comparisons with previous performance seems justifiable. The percentage of minority enrollment by school site for the six-year period is as follows:

	1970	1971	1972	1973	1974	1975
Site A	7.6	10.0	9.6	11.1	8.2	10.0
Site B	12.6	8.5	12.5	14.3	16.0	16.6
Site C	7.9	10.3	10.2	13.1	15.9	19.3
Site D	14.8	19.5	20.7	19.9	23.7	16.1

Nevertheless, the future for these schools does not appear too promising because radical changes in racial balance are anticipated along with a significant influx of low achievers. The collegial team concept is thus being used in these schools to help teachers meet this challenge and to place incentives toward a more functional division of labor.

Three of the school sites experimented with earlier versions of the collegial team concept in 1974, the year prior to the model study year. These previous experiments, conducted with smaller numbers of students, produced the following results in terms of percentage of achieved goals:

	1974	1975
Site A	50.3%	48.6%
Site B	52.2%	55.0%
Site C	47.4%	51.0%

The districtwide average goal met was 39 for 1974 and 37 for 1975; thus, the collegial team schools averaged higher performance than the rest of the school district. This fact tends to demonstrate how the marginal cost of teaching is increasing in the district or, stated differently, teaching is becoming more difficult.

Methodology for Long-Range Assessment

A major problem with most educational evaluations of innovative programs is that long-range assessment of cognitive growth is neglected. The purpose of this discussion is to illustrate how the collegial team innovation can be evaluated for long-range effects in terms of cognitive growth. First, in order to assess any long-range impacts of a particular educational innovation, attention must be given to probability estimates of future cognitive growth such as reading grade level, given a present reading grade level or grade equivalent score.

Using a random sample of student cognitive measures, it was possible to construct tables showing the probability of a future level of cognitive growth given the present grade level. Tables 3-1 through 3-3 show the probability distribution of fifth-grade scores given fourth-grade scores of $4\pm.1$ grade equivalent; similarly, Tables 3-4 through 3-6 show the sixth-grade scores; and finally, Tables 3-7 through 3-9 present seventh-grade scores, given fourth-grade scores. An analysis is presented for different cognitive areas, including reading, language arts, and mathematics.

From these tables it is apparent that if a student is reading from 3.9 to 4.1 in the fourth grade, his chances are less than .5 that he will be reading at 7.5 in the seventh grade. For language arts, if he is performing in the range 3.9 to 4.1 in grade 4, the .5 level is 7.0. For math, under the same conditions, it is 6.3.

Note also from these tables that as the time horizon increases, the percentage of students at grade level or higher decreases, especially in mathematics. This analysis is summarized in Table 3-10.

In short, the problem of accurately predicting future scores of students is an extremely difficult and complex task. A procedure based upon Bayesian analysis can be employed to examine the long-range effects of the collegial team concept. First, by using state department of education or school district records, one can easily find, for example, the prediction of seventh-grade scores from grade 4. Using $P(4|7)$ and $P(7)$, where $P(4|7)$ means the probability distribution of seventh-grade scores, given a student's score in the fourth grade; one can give a probabilistic assessment of a student's future performance given his past performance. $P(4)$, or the probability distribution of fourth-grade scores, can then be derived from the formula:

$$P(4) = \Sigma P(4|7)\ P(7).$$

Then using Bayes' theorem:

$$P(7|4) = \frac{P(4|7)\ P(7)}{P(4)}.$$

$P(7)$ can then be varied to reflect characteristics of a particular school or school district.

This stochastic methodology can be built into a treatment-control group experimental design or a colleague-noncolleague team school to provide a long-range probabilistic assessment of the treat-

Table 3-1
Probability Distribution of Fifth-Grade Reading Scores, Given an Observed Score of 4 $\mp$ .1 in Fourth Grade P(5|4)

Grade Equiv	Probability	Cumulative Probability
2.30	0.01	0.01
2.50	0.01	0.01
2.70	0.01	0.02
3.00	0.02	0.04
3.30	0.03	0.07
3.50	0.03	0.10
4.10	0.01	0.11
4.20	0.01	0.11
4.30	0.03	0.14
4.50	0.01	0.15
4.60	0.01	0.16
4.70	0.03	0.19
4.80	0.04	0.23
5.00	0.04	0.26
5.10	0.03	0.29
5.20	0.01	0.30
5.30	0.04	0.34
5.50	0.10	0.44
5.60	0.09	0.53
5.70	0.03	0.56
5.80	0.05	0.61
6.00	0.03	0.64
6.10	0.04	0.67
6.20	0.04	0.71
6.30	0.04	0.74
6.50	0.11	0.85
6.60	0.01	0.86
6.70	0.03	0.89
6.80	0.03	0.92
7.00	0.02	0.94
7.10	0.02	0.96
7.20	0.01	0.98
7.30	0.01	0.99
7.60	0.01	0.99
7.80	0.01	1.00

ment. One procedure could be to examine posttest scores shown in experimental and control groups and to note the expected number, based upon scores in grade 1, which would be achieving at or above grade level (or any other cutoff) in grade $i + 1$ or any other future time period. A Chi-square analysis could then be used to see whether the treatment group registers statistically significant more students who would be at or above grade level in the specified future time period. Schematically, this experimental design can be described as in Figure 3-1.

Table 3-2
Probability Distribution of Fifth-Grade Scores in Language Arts, Given an Observed Score of 4 ∓ .1 in Fourth Grade P(5|4)

Grade Equiv	Probability	Cumulative Probability
2.50	0.02	0.02
2.80	0.02	0.03
4.00	0.02	0.05
4.10	0.02	0.06
4.30	0.02	0.08
4.50	0.08	0.15
4.60	0.03	0.18
4.70	0.05	0.23
4.80	0.11	0.34
5.00	0.10	0.44
5.20	0.08	0.52
5.30	0.05	0.57
5.50	0.10	0.67
5.60	0.03	0.70
5.80	0.02	0.72
6.00	0.02	0.74
6.10	0.04	0.78
6.20	0.05	0.83
6.50	0.03	0.86
6.60	0.02	0.88
6.70	0.04	0.92
6.80	0.02	0.94
7.00	0.02	0.96
7.10	0.02	0.98
7.20	0.02	0.99
7.50	0.01	1.00

The procedure can now be used directly to systematically investigate the long-range impact of collegial teams upon students. For example, what is the difference between P(7|4) for students taught by a collegial team as opposed to those not taught by a collegial team? One might find that a child taught by a collegial team in grade 4, at say, 4.0. grade equivalent will have less than a 50 percent chance of reaching grade equivalent level in seventh grade, while a nonteam-taught child reading at an identical level would have less than a 30 percent chance. Through these indirect probabilistic assessments, one might also find the effects of schooling and instructional programs. By considering per pupil cost of instructional programs in the analysis, interesting economic benefit-cost analysis can also be pursued, and tradeoffs using expected value theory can be performed (cost times probability to attain a goal). Thus, by analyzing, after three years of data are collected, the probability distribution of, for example, seventh-grade reading scores given the third-grade reading score, one will be better able to assess whether or not the collegial team concept statistically affects the distribution of future reading scores when present scores are given.

Table 3-3
Probability Distribution of Fifth-Grade Scores in Mathematics, Given an Observed Score of 4 $\mp$ .1 in Fourth Grade P(5|4)

Grade Equiv	Probability	Cumulative Probability
2.20	0.02	0.02
2.30	0.02	0.03
2.50	0.01	0.04
2.70	0.06	0.10
3.00	0.05	0.15
3.20	0.07	0.22
3.50	0.04	0.26
3.80	0.05	0.31
4.00	0.14	0.44
4.30	0.14	0.58
4.60	0.14	0.72
4.80	0.06	0.76
5.10	0.04	0.82
5.20	0.05	0.86
5.30	0.04	0.90
5.60	0.03	0.93
5.70	0.02	0.95
6.00	0.03	0.98
6.10	0.01	0.98
6.30	0.01	0.99
6.50	0.01	1.00

Table 3-4
Probability Distribution of Sixth-Grade Reading Scores, Given an Observed Score of 4 $\mp$ .1 in Fourth Grade P(6|4)

Grade Equiv	Probability	Cumulative Probability
2.10	0.01	0.01
3.50	0.01	0.01
4.10	0.01	0.02
4.30	0.01	0.03
4.50	0.01	0.04
4.70	0.01	0.05
4.80	0.01	0.06
5.00	0.05	0.11
5.20	0.02	0.13
5.30	0.02	0.15
5.50	0.05	0.20
5.60	0.01	0.21

Grade Equiv	Probability	Cumulative Probability
5.70	0.04	0.25
5.80	0.04	0.29
6.00	0.02	0.31
6.10	0.04	0.34
6.20	0.04	0.39
6.30	0.04	0.43
6.50	0.06	0.49
6.60	0.03	0.52
6.70	0.05	0.57
6.80	0.06	0.64
7.00	0.05	0.69
7.10	0.02	0.71
7.20	0.06	0.77
7.30	0.01	0.78
7.50	0.03	0.81
7.60	0.01	0.81
7.70	0.03	0.84
7.80	0.02	0.86
8.00	0.01	0.87
8.10	0.01	0.89
8.20	0.04	0.92
8.30	0.03	0.95
8.50	0.02	0.97
8.60	0.01	0.99
9.00	0.01	0.99
9.60	0.01	1.00
6.30	0.04	0.55
6.50	0.10	0.65

Table 3-5
Probability Distribution of Sixth-Grade Scores in Language Arts, Given an Observed Score of 4 ∓ .1 in Fourth Grade P(6|4)

Grade Equiv	Probability	Cumulative Probability
2.70	0.01	0.01
3.20	0.02	0.02
3.80	0.02	0.04
4.20	0.01	0.05
4.30	0.01	0.05
4.80	0.05	0.10
5.10	0.02	0.12
5.20	0.05	0.17
5.30	0.06	0.23
5.50	0.03	0.27
5.60	0.06	0.33
5.70	0.04	0.36
5.80	0.03	0.39
6.00	0.09	0.48
6.10	0.02	0.50
6.20	0.02	0.52

Table 3-5 (cont.)

Grade Equiv	Probability	Cumulative Probability
6.60	0.03	0.68
6.70	0.03	0.71
6.80	0.02	0.73
7.00	0.06	0.80
7.10	0.03	0.83
7.20	0.02	0.85
7.30	0.01	0.86
7.50	0.05	0.90
7.70	0.01	0.91
7.80	0.02	0.92
8.00	0.01	0.93
8.10	0.01	0.94
8.20	0.01	0.95
8.30	0.01	0.95
8.50	0.01	0.96
8.80	0.02	0.98
9.00	0.02	0.99
9.50	0.01	1.00

Table 3-6
Probability Distribution of Sixth-Grade Scores in Mathematics, Given an Observed Score of 4 $\mp$ .1 in Fourth Grade P(6|4)

Grade Equiv	Probability	Cumulative Probability
2.80	0.01	0.01
3.20	0.01	0.02
3.30	0.02	0.04
3.50	0.01	0.05
3.70	0.02	0.07
4.00	0.02	0.09
4.10	0.02	0.11
4.20	0.02	0.13
4.50	0.05	0.18
4.70	0.02	0.20
4.80	0.04	0.24
5.00	0.05	0.28
5.10	0.03	0.31
5.20	0.05	0.37
5.30	0.02	0.38
5.50	0.09	0.47
5.60	0.14	0.61
5.70	0.05	0.66
6.00	0.09	0.75
6.20	0.02	0.77
6.30	0.04	0.81

Grade Equiv	Probability	Cumulative Probability
6.50	0.07	0.88
6.60	0.01	0.89
6.70	0.01	0.89
6.80	0.01	0.90
7.00	0.02	0.92
7.10	0.04	0.96
7.20	0.02	0.98
7.50	0.01	0.98
7.70	0.01	0.99
8.60	0.01	1.00

Table 3-7
Probability Distribution of Seventh-Grade Reading Scores, Given an Observed Score of 4 $\mp$ .1 in Fourth Grade P(7|4)

Grave Equiv	Probability	Cumulative Probability
5.60	0.01	0.01
5.80	0.01	0.03
6.00	0.01	0.04
6.10	0.01	0.05
6.20	0.01	0.06
6.30	0.01	0.07
6.50	0.03	0.10
6.60	0.04	0.14
6.70	0.04	0.18
6.80	0.01	0.19
7.00	0.05	0.24
7.10	0.06	0.30
7.20	0.06	0.36
7.30	0.03	0.39
7.50	0.10	0.49
7.60	0.04	0.53
7.70	0.04	0.56
7.80	0.05	0.61
8.00	0.07	0.69
8.10	0.03	0.71
8.20	0.03	0.74
8.30	0.02	0.76
8.50	0.07	0.84
8.60	0.02	0.86
8.70	0.01	0.86
9.00	0.01	0.88
9.10	0.02	0.90
9.20	0.02	0.92
9.50	0.01	0.94
9.60	0.02	0.96
10.70	0.01	0.97
11.00	0.01	0.98

Table 3-8
Probability Distribution of Seventh-Grade Language Arts Scores, Given an Observed Score of 4 $\mp$ .1 in Fourth Grade P(7|4)

Grade Equiv	Probability	Cumulative Probability
4.30	0.02	0.02
4.70	0.01	0.02
4.80	0.01	0.03
5.00	0.02	0.05
5.10	0.02	0.07
5.50	0.02	0.09
5.60	0.02	0.11
5.70	0.02	0.13
5.80	0.02	0.15
6.00	0.03	0.18
6.10	0.01	0.19
6.20	0.05	0.23
6.30	0.04	0.27
6.50	0.05	0.32
6.60	0.01	0.33
6.70	0.03	0.36
6.80	0.06	0.42
7.00	0.07	0.48
7.10	0.03	0.52
7.20	0.01	0.52
7.30	0.05	0.58
7.50	0.08	0.66
7.70	0.02	0.68
7.80	0.05	0.73
8.00	0.03	0.77
8.10	0.02	0.78
8.20	0.02	0.80
8.30	0.02	0.81
8.50	0.02	0.83
8.60	0.02	0.85
8.70	0.04	0.89
9.00	0.02	0.91
9.10	0.02	0.93
9.30	0.03	0.96
9.60	0.01	0.97
10.00	0.01	0.98
10.20	0.01	0.98
10.50	0.01	0.99

Table 3-9
Probability Distribution of Seventh-Grade Scores in Mathematics, Given an Observed Score of 4 $\mp$ .1 in Fourth Grade P(7|4)

Grade Equiv	Probability	Cumulative Probability
2.60	0.01	0.01
3.30	0.01	0.02
3.50	0.01	0.02

Grade Equiv	Probability	Cumulative Probability
3.70	0.01	0.03
4.20	0.01	0.04
4.50	0.01	0.05
4.70	0.02	0.06
4.80	0.01	0.07
5.00	0.03	0.10
5.10	0.04	0.14
5.20	0.01	0.15
5.50	0.06	0.21
5.60	0.04	0.24
5.70	0.03	0.27
6.00	0.08	0.36
6.20	0.03	0.39
6.30	0.08	0.47
6.50	0.15	0.62
6.60	0.05	0.67
6.80	0.01	0.68
7.00	0.04	0.72
7.10	0.08	0.80
7.20	0.01	0.81
7.50	0.05	0.86
7.60	0.02	0.88
7.70	0.02	0.90
8.00	0.02	0.92
8.10	0.03	0.95
8.50	0.02	0.97
8.60	0.02	0.98
9.00	0.01	0.99

Table 3-10

Percentage of Students at or Above Grade Level at Grades 5, 6 and 7, Given that They Were at Grade Level in Grade 4

	Grades		
	5	6	7
Reading	.74	.69	.75
Mathematics	.18	.25	.20
Language Arts	.56	.52	.52

Summary

In summary, the initial evaluation phase of the collegial team concept demonstrated that schools employing this concept seem to

	Number at target G.E. level or higher	Number projected higher than future target G.E. level
Experimental Group		
Control Group		

Figure 3-1. Experimental Design Using Probabilistic Assessment Method

outperform, on a one-by-one student basis, those schools not utilizing this method of organizing the instructional program. Of course, with a sample size of only four school sites and with some variations in the leadership styles of the principals, it would be impossible to test statistically the validity of the concept. However, in studies of this type, educational significance or the ratio of performance gains to per pupil cost takes precedence over statistical significance. In addition, the collegial team concept has been shown capable of providing economic incentives for solving a multitude of problems facing school officials. In the model study presented here, approximately 300 students per school had more access to and attention from the teacher team with less than $10.00 additional cost per average daily attendance (ADA), which thus indicates that the concept seems viable from an economic viewpoint. (Note actual cost to the district in the way of additional compensation was less than $5.00 per student.)

In the second section of this chapter, a methodology was proposed for extensive long-range evaluation of the technique. Here the probability distribution of future cognitive growth scores were examined to see whether they were biased toward pupils who were taught under the collegial team. In sum, the institutional profit sharing in the form of the bonuses given school sites A, B, C, and D is a radical concept in education and of course must be permitted a breaking in period before teachers can develop their own particular organizational structure to maximize their earnings. On basis of the evidence gathered to this date, the placing of incentives towards the slower learners seems to have its intended effect, namely, greater teacher effort for these students. The students and parents, of course, should endorse the concept purely on practical grounds since it places financial incentives toward their self interests. What about teachers? What are their views concerning institutional profit sharing? How does the collegial team concept translate itself in terms of teacher evaluation and teacher professionalism? The next chapter presents empirical evidence collected from teachers operating as collegial teams and those operating in traditional classroom assignments.

4

Evaluating Teacher Behavior

Educators would agree that the essential link in the implementation of any innovation in the classroom is the teacher. It is no mystery that educational innovations not responsive to the needs of teachers have little chance of being accepted and established in the schools. As mentioned in Chapter 1, the key feature of the collegial team concept is its design to increase the professionalism of teachers by giving them a greater voice in decision making and evaluation. The extent to which collegial teams affect individual teacher behavior in this area thus becomes an extremely important element in the way collegial teams are evaluated in a school district.

The purpose of this chapter is specifically to examine the effects of the collegial team concept on teacher attitude and behavior in the areas of curriculum decision making, evaluation, professionalism, and collective bargaining. Obviously, due to sample size limitations, very little can be said statistically concerning the magnitudes of these differences. Yet, the directions of these differences seem to favor the collegial team concept. A methodology is proposed at the conclusion of the chapter to examine the effects of the collegial team concept on various dimensions of teacher behavior. This methodology could be used by school districts to examine statistically the attitudinal effects of the collegial team concept on teachers in the district.

Preliminary Findings

To accomplish the task of evaluating the effect of the collegial team on teacher behavior, a questionnaire was developed to solicit teacher reaction in the areas mentioned above. This questionnaire, which can be found in Appendix B, was administered to teachers in both experimental and control groups.

In the area of curriculum decision making, teacher reaction to the questionnaire statements below was sought by asking them to respond on a strongly disagree to strongly agree (1-5) scale. The

63

following statements apply to the teachers' perceptions of what teachers *should* do:

1. If teachers are involved in curriculum decision making, they are less likely to be involved in activities that might lead to sanctions or lockouts.
2. Having teachers involved in curriculum decision making would result in higher cognitive growth for students.
4. A strategy for increasing the professionalism of teachers would be to have teachers involved in all aspects of curricular decisions.

The statements below apply to their perception of what teachers *actually* do:

22. Teachers are heavily involved in curriculum decision making.
28. There is a serious teacher morale problem since teachers do not have a voice in decision making.
32. Teachers are left alone to make all decisions related to instruction.
38. Teachers are centrally involved in making major educational policy decisions.

Statements 1, 2, and 4 refer to teacher perceptions of schools and ideal teacher behavior in general, while statements 22, 28, 32, and 38 refer to teacher opinions concerning what is apparent or actually happening at their own particular schools. The means and standard deviations for both the collegial and noncollegial team groups are reported below:

Statement Number	Mean Score	Overall Standard Deviation	Nonteam Mean	Collegial Team Mean Score
1	2.06	.8	2.1	1.9
2	1.68	.7	1.6	1.7
4	3.9	.8	1.6	2.1
22	2.6	1.0	2.7	2.8
28	3.04	1.2	3.5	3.4
32	4.1	1.1	3.9	4.0
38	3.2	1.0	3.0	3.5
Average Age of Teachers	34	14	34	35

These results clearly point out that in general there is high similarity in the way teachers in collegial and noncollegial troups responded to those questions, with slightly higher variations in the responses (higher standard deviation) related to what is actual practice at the school site. Because some principals (in the control schools) had already provided teachers with a greater voice in curriculum decision making, the differences are not large between team and non-team teachers. The average of teachers in both groups was also found to be similar. In the key statement of the group (item 38), which states that teachers are centrally involved in making *major* educational policy decisions, there is a large difference in favor of collegial teams. Much encouragement was given to collegial team teachers in this important area of responsibility.

As noted earlier, teacher evaluation is perhaps the most onerous task for school administrators and typically forms the basis for a large amount of the discord found in school districts. The following questionnaire statements apply to this important dimension:

3. Teacher evaluation of each other is an excellent mechanism for increasing overall teaching performance.
5. For increasing professionalism among teachers, it is important that teachers are involved in the evaluation of each other rather than leaving evaluation strictly to administrators.
10. There are teachers who could and should be helped in terms of improving their teaching performance but they are neglected because there is no incentive.
11. Only fellow teachers can help improve the teaching performance of other teachers.
23. Teachers evaluate other teachers for the purpose of improving teaching performance.
27. There is no need for teachers to give advice to other teachers for improving teaching performance because all are equally competent.
36. Teachers know who the poor performing teachers are.
37. Every effort is made to assist poor performing teachers.

Note that statements 3, 5, 10, and 11 refer to teacher perceptions in general, while 23, 27, 36, and 37 refer to actual conditions at the particular school site. The means and standard deviations are reported below:

Statement Number	Mean Score	Overall Standard Deviation	Nonteam Mean Score	Collegial Team Mean Score
3	3.4	1.3	3.6	3.1
5	3.3	1.3	3.0	3.5
10	2.9	1.1	2.9	2.8
11	3.8	.9	3.6	3.9
23	3.3	.9	3.2	3.3
27	4.2	1.3	4.2	4.3
36	2.2	.95	2.0	2.5
37	3.2	1.2	3.3	3.1

From question 36, it is interesting to note that teachers are aware of and able to identify the poorer performing teachers in their schools. In a collegial setting, they accept some responsibility for this problem.

Teachers on the collegial team felt that teacher evaluation of each other was an excellent mechanism for increasing teacher performance; however, there was a great deal of variation (standard deviation 1.3) among all the teachers sampled. In general, collegial team teachers were more committed to teachers' helping other teachers than nonteam teachers. One reason might be that the collegial team concept is based upon shared teacher performance and evaluation.

Demands for increased professionalism in the teaching profession has resulted in many conflicts between school administrators and teachers. The struggle between the "professional attitude" and the "union collective bargaining attitude" has caused much dissension within the teaching ranks. The questionnaire statements below were designed to elicit attitudes toward professionalism among teachers:

4. A strategy for increasing the professionalism of teachers would be to have teachers involved in all aspects of curricular decisions.

5. For increasing professionalism among teachers, it is important that teachers are involved in the evaluation of each other rather than leaving evaluation strictly to administrators.

13. In terms of teacher support, it would be better to have a "group" profit-sharing plan for an entire school rather than have individual merit pay for teachers.

17. Teachers are happiest and most content when they are treated as professionals when it comes to evaluation and decision making.

19. Probationary teachers should be granted tenure only upon the recommendation of the permanent teachers.
20. A teacher should practice his ideas on what is best for students even though the administration prefers other methods.
21. To do his best, a teacher needs to know what is going on in the whole school.
31. The administrators interfere with what teachers know is the best way to teach children.
33. Permanent teachers are heavily involved in the hiring of new staff and granting of tenure.
34. The administrator consults teachers on class scheduling, teacher assignments, transfer plans, discipline, promotion, and instructional loads.
35. Teachers are in constant communication with each other and know what other teachers are doing.

The means and standard deviation, both for the group as a whole and the collegial team and nonteam groups are reported below:

Statement Number	Mean Score	Standard Deviation	Nonteam Mean Score	Collegial Team Mean Score
4	1.9	.8	1.6	2.1
5	3.3	1.3	3.0	3.5
13	2.8	1.1	2.5	3.0
17	3.3	.62	3.2	3.5
19	2.6	1.2	3.5	3.3
21	2.8	1.1	1.5	2.5
31	3.6	.97	3.7	3.7
33	4.1	1.1	4.1	4.1
34	2.1	1.1	1.7	2.5
35	2.4	.96	2.4	2.4

The generally higher scores of collegial team teachers in this set of statements indicates an endorsement of the collegial team concept as a means toward higher levels of professional behavior. The endorsement is particularly valuable to school policy analysts concerned with the current increase in teacher militancy. Notice also that the least variation (standard deviation .62) occurs in response to the statement that teachers are happiest and most content when they are treated as professionals when it comes to evaluation and decision making. Both groups gave this statement high endorsement.

Another important design criteria for the collegial team concept is its attention to the slow, difficult-to-teach child. The nonlinear marginal cost curve reflects the fact that some students are easier to teach than others, hence rewards are not based upon a uniform measure but upon a differential measure commensurate with difficulty. The following set of statements were used to indicate whether or not proper attention is being given to slower students:

6. Some students are "left out" in the classroom because they require an inordinate amount of attention from the teacher.
7. If a teacher is to be evaluated on classroom performance, it is better for teachers to work with the good and average students and to spend less time and effort struggling with the slower students.
8. Some students do not receive their fair share of instructional resources from the teacher.
16. Student learning is better served when teams of teachers are involved together in instruction and evaluation.
25. Some students, because they are slowere, do not get the attention they need.
26. Slower students get commensurately more teacher attention than fast students.

The following are the means and standard deviations for the whole group and for the team and nonteam members:

Statement Number	Mean Score	Standard Deviation	Nonteam Mean Score	Collegial Team Mean Score
6	2.8	1.1	2.5	3.1
7	3.5	1.2	3.5	3.4
8	2.9	1.2	3.2	2.6
16	2.3	.91	2.0	2.5
25	3.5	1.2	3 6	3.6
26	3.1	1.2	3.4	2.7

One of the principal objectives of the collegial team concept and the nonlinear payment schedule is to increase the attention of teachers toward the needs of poorly achieving students. The responses to these questions seems to confirm the view that teachers understand those needs in all schools. Incentives that reward attention to such students could capitalize on that understanding. In general the nonteam teachers consistently understated the problem of slow learners in the classroom. On one hand, nonteam teachers felt that some students do not receive their fair share of instructional resources from the teacher (statement 8: mean 3.2 for nonteam; 2.6 for team), but then agreed with the statement that slower students get more attention than fast students (question 26: mean 3.4 for nonteam; 2.7 for team).Probably there was some defensiveness on the part of these nonteam teachers concerning their behavior toward slower students, because such students focus greater attention and concern in schools.

The following series of statements were used in the questionnaire to elicit attitudes on the important issue of collective bargaining in the schools:

14. The primary reason teachers consider striking is monetary.
15. The primary reason teachers consider striking is because the conditions of learning and the conditions under which a teacher is evaluated are poor.
18. If school administrators could get away with it, they would probably increase the work load of teachers.
19. Probationary teachers should be granted tenure only upon the recommendation of the permanent teachers.
20. A teacher should practice his ideas on what is best for students even though the administration prefers other methods.
24. Teachers at our school are less militant than those at other schools.
29. Teachers at our school are unhappy with the school district for reasons more centered around the instructional system than for more money.

The following are the means and standard deviations for the whole group and team and nonteam members:

Statement Number	Mean Score	Standard Deviation	Nonteam Mean Score	Collegial Team Mean Score
14	3.3	1.3	3.2	3.5
15	2.6	.9	2.2	2.9
18	3.3	1.1	3.1	3.5
19	3.4	1.3	3.5	3.3
20	2.6	1.1	2.5	2.6
24	2.1	.88	1.8	2.3
29	3.0	1.2	2.7	3.4

The relationship of responses between regular and collegial team teachers is not significantly different in this subset of questions. Although consistent with other research evidence, teacher militancy is not uniform across schools in a district. In this situation, the collegial team group seemed to be less militant (question 24: mean 1.8 for nonteam schools; 2.3 for team schools) than the nonteam schools. The responses to the statements tend to follow the patterns one would expect. Note the results for item 29 (teachers at our school are unhappy with the school district more for reasons centered around the institutional system than for money) were mean 2.7 for nonteam and 3.4 for collegial team schools. The following statements were used to measure general teacher attitudes:

30. Teachers often use the instructional resources of the school district such as curriculum specialists, media centers and other central office services.

31. The administrators interfere with what teachers know is the best way to teach children.

32. Teachers are left alone to make all decisions related to instruction.

The means and standard deviations for the whole group and collegial team and nonteam teachers were as follows:

Statement Number	Group Mean Score	Nonteam Mean Score	Collegial Team Mean Score
30	2.5	2.6	2.3
31	3.6	3.7	3.6
32	3.9	3.9	3.9

On these statements there was very little difference between regular and collegial team teachers. Notice both groups have generally high endorsements to question 32 (teachers, if left alone, could make all decisions related to instruction) with the mean for both groups being 3.9.

In summary, these preliminary findings suggest that the collegial team concept is beginning to have its intended effect in the area of teacher evaluation, curriculum decision making, and professionalism in the model study schools. Obviously, due to both time limitations of operation and small sample sizes, statistical confidence cannot be established. In addition, the collegial team teachers seem to have different perceptions concerning professionalism than the nonteam teachers (measures on the initial set, 1-20, of questions).

Since the collegial team was a self-selected group, we would expect these differences. Finally, because many of the control teachers came from the same school site and the influence on the teachers by style of the principal was the same, the differences in the responses to questions dealing with instruction and slower students attention between team and nonteam teachers was small. Hence these small differences might have been understated between team and nonteam teachers. With larger samples across different districts, these differences would undoubtedly be much greater.

Taken one at a time, these statements do not seem to show any consistent difference between team and nonteam members. Taken as a group in a multivariate manner, however, we can examine statistically whether these groups, team and nonteam teachers, are consistently different and furthermore indicate which questions best discriminate between the two groups. The next section proposes a methodology that a school district might employ to determine whether the collegial team concept is having its effect in terms of desired changes in teacher attitudes and behavior.

Methodology for Assessing Teacher Changes

In attempting to show that teacher attitudes and behavior with the collegial team approach is statistically different from teacher behavior and attitudes in traditional classroom units, more advanced statistical methods must be used.

The methodology proposed for the evaluation of the teacher component of the collegial team approach is multivariate discriminant analysis. With one group being teachers on the collegial teams and the other group being regular classroom teachers, this technique systematically examines which responses to the attitude questionnaire significantly discriminate between the regular teaching and collegial team teaching groups. Questions 22 through 39 reflected the responses of each group concerning what was actually happening at their own particular schools. Below are the means for each group, as well as the overall group mean, for the items on the teacher attitude questionnaire that were directed at finding what actually is happening as opposed to what should happen at the school sites.

Question	Group Control	Team 1	Overall Mean
22	2.7	2.8	2.7
23	3.2	3.3	3.2
24	1.8	2.3	2.1
25	3.6	3.5	3.5
26	3.3	2.7	3.0
27	4.2	4.2	4.2
28	3.5	3.2	3.4
29	2.7	3.4	3.0
30	2.6	2.2	2.4
31	3.7	3.6	3.6
32	3.9	3.9	3.9
33	4.1	4.0	4.1
34	1.7	2.5	2.1
35	2.4	2.4	2.4
36	2.0	2.5	2.2
37	3.3	3.0	3.2
38	3.2	3.0	3.5
39	3.3	3.3	3.3

The standard deviations for these groups on these questions are reported below.

Question	Group Control	Team 1
22	1.0	1.0
23	1.2	0.8
24	0.8	0.7
25	1.3	1.1
26	1.1	1.1
27	0.5	0.6
28	1.3	1.1
29	1.2	1.0
30	1.1	1.0
31	0.9	0.9
32	0.7	0.6
33	0.9	1.2
34	0.7	1.2
35	0.9	0.9
36	0.8	0.9
37	0.8	1.0
38	1.0	1.3
39	0.8	1.2

The stepwise discriminant procedure finds those variables, or questionnaire items, in order of importance, which discriminate collegial team teachers from nonteam members along the set of attitudes and behaviors indicated by the items on the questionnaire. The most significant questions that discriminate between collegial team teachers versus regular teachers were in order of importance found to be:

Question	Univariate F values
34	13.4
29	18.4
37	5.2
26	7.3
27	12.8
38	6.1
30	4.5
24	2.5

The model achieved a statistically significant discrimination between team and nonteam teachers ($F = 4.9$; $P < .05$)—that is, taken as a multivariate distribution of all questions (22-39), there was a statistically different distribution of team and nonteam teacher responses to the questions.

The mathematical function that maximizes this discrimination tells how the variables must be weighted in order to achieve maximum discrimination or for the distributions to be maximally dispersed. The discrimination function separating teachers into the two groups was:

Question	Control Group	Treatment Group
22	5.7	5.6
23	2.5	2.6
24	-2.7	-1.8
25	-2.7	-2.8
26	-0.6	-2.0
27	21.7	24.4
28	2.0	1.8
29	5.0	6.6
30	5.2	5.4
31	9.2	8.9
32	15.7	17.0
33	2.8	3.3
34	11.9	13.8
35	-6.0	-6.4
36	4.5	4.7
37	2.8	1.6
38	-0.2	-1.6
39	1.7	1.6
Constant	-135.8	-150.4

The questions that successfully distinguish between the collegial team schools and regular schools are, in order of importance:

34. The administrator consults teachers on class scheduling, teacher assignments, transfer plans, discipline, promotion and instructional loads.

29. Teachers at our school are unhappy with the school district

more for reasons centered around the instructional system than for more money.

37. Every effort is made to assist poor performing teachers.

26. Slower students get commensurately more teacher attention than fast students.

27. There is no need for teachers to give advice to other teachers for improving teaching performance because all are equally competent.

38. Teachers are centrally involved in making major educational policy decisions.

30. Teachers often use the instructional resources of the school district such as curriculum specialists, media centers and other central office services.

24. Teachers at our school are less militant than those at other schools.

31. The administrators interfere with what teachers know is the best way to teach children.

32. Teachers are left alone to make all decisions related to instruction.

The findings of this preliminary analysis using the discriminant function methodology indicates that many of the objectives of the collegial team—such as effort to assist poor performing teachers, giving slower students commensurately more attention, and less militant teacher behavior—are being met.

In fact, the order of importance of responses resulting in the discrimination between the team and nonteam groups corresponds exactly with what the collegial team hopes to accomplish at the school site: namely greater teacher voice in decision making; overcoming educational performance impediments by assisting poor performing teachers; and getting more teacher attention to slower students or to students who were formerly left out of the instructional process.

Summary

In summary, the fact that differences between experimental and control group teachers is small suggests that a general readiness for the collegial concept exists among teachers. Their awareness of the problems that exist in the present system makes them amenable to a change strategy that would address the problems identified.

In effect, teachers feel that they should be involved in curriculum decision making. A collegial team is by definition involved in program evaluation. Because programs (reading, mathematics, art, social studies) make up the curriculum and teachers implement the programs with students, curriculum decisions made by others too often result in lack of teacher commitment. The result is a chaotic program lacking continuity and sequence over time. Students, particularly those who find learning most difficult, suffer in such a system. Their learning is thwarted.

The questionnaire items concerning teacher evaluation again revealed that teachers may be more amenable to a collegial involvement in that process than administrators realize or are willing to admit. A strategy that allows teachers to select among a wide variety of evaluation data sources so that the individual threat potential is reduced would promote a professional peer relationship based upon the improvement of group performance. This condition tends to move the poor performing teacher toward the excellent teacher in an atmosphere of trust and mutual support.

Questionnaire items concerning teacher attitudes on collective bargaining versus professionalism tended to confirm that teachers prefer the professional role. The divisive movement toward a union stance in education is a creature of events and not a product of teacher preference. The collegial team concept provides an acceptable alternative to the union movement that could reunite a system that has been pushing itself in a direction anathema to teachers, administrators, boards of education, and the public at large.

Questionnaire items concerning students who are most difficult to teach seemed to confirm that teachers are very aware of the needs of these students. Their frustrations in dealing effectively with such students can be ameliorated in a collegial setting. Learning problems in a typical classroom are generally too diverse and complex for adequate treatment by the strategies one mind can devise. Teachers need the combined brain power of their colleagues to systematically address the needs of their students. A collegial team setting provides a mechanism for addressing that need.

Teachers, of course, are the critical element in the successful implementation of the collegial team concept. Despite the small amount of time teachers had to adapt themselves to such a radically different way of organizing the instructional delivery system, they not only seemed to endorse the overall concepts, but specifically endorsed the many design features in the collegial team. However, a moderate period of readjustment would seem to be required to derive the full benefits of the collegial team concept.

With student input moving towards a lower quality (due to declining birth rates, especially from high socioeconomic-status parents), thereby resulting in higher marginal cost for teachers to maintain the same levels of cognitive outputs, and with a trend toward a collective bargaining militant posture, a concept such as collegial teams might well assist educational policy makers in meeting these future challenges.

Because of the problems mentioned earlier, namely small sample size, time period for establishing procedures, articulation of the concept, and so forth, it is inappropriate to evaluate such a radical departure from present school procedures purely on statistical empirical evidence. Even with these limitations, however, the data does generally support the overall effectiveness of the collegial team in meeting its design specifications from the viewpoint of both teachers and students. Anecdotal information provided by teachers and principals are most significant in completing the evaluation of the collegial team. This information is found in the next chapter.

In summary, the proposed methodologies, bayesian analysis, and stepwise multivariate discriminant analysis can be used by school officials interested in examining the statistical efficacy of the collegial team concept in their own districts. They were presented in these last two chapters to illustrate how empirical statistical evaluation can be systematically conducted to evaluate the concept and its effects upon pupil performance and teacher attitudes. In view of the low per pupil cost (less than $5/ADA) and the performance increase demonstrated, certainly the collegial team concept is worthwhile from a benefit-cost standpoint and is an excellent innovation for consideration by school districts desiring a means for restructuring their educational system.

5

Collegial Team Schools in Operation

The Schools

The experimental schools reported on here are located in an upward mobil, middle socioeconomic area. The schools are all average in size (500 to 700 students), and the minority population (primarily Spanish surname) is in the 10 to 15 percent range. The district as a whole has experienced a significant enrollment decline. Because the tax base is composed of primarily residential components, the assessed value is low and the tax rate high. The district is included in the "low wealth" category among all unified districts in California. The amount spent per child for the current cost of education was approximately $860 in 1974. The district serves a population of approximately 150,000 people and has a student population, K-12, of approximately 26,000.

Schools A, B, and C are K-6 schools. School D is an intermediate school for grades 7 and 8. The faculties of each school are typical for the district in terms of age, experience and training. All teachers, except one, among the four teams have tenure. They are generally a stable, mature, and experienced group of teachers with no special characteristics to set them apart from the teaching staff in most schools.

The schools used to test the collegial team schema were not selected. Their principals volunteered to participate in the experimental work after the model had been explained to all principals in the district. Having volunteered their schools, these principals would be expected to be favorably disposed to the collegial team plan and interested in contributing to its success. Their teachers were more skeptical, so that a presentation on the rationale for collegial teams was presented by the authors to each group. Since there appeared to be nothing to lose by participating, resistance in the teacher groups at each school receded rapidly.

The interval shift analysis portion of the experiment was negotiated in terms that made it obvious that the team could not lose

77

with respect to the incentive reward. If half their students achieved one grade equivalent of growth, they would receive a $500 incentive team grant. If the objective was reached with 90 percent of their students, they would gain $1,500 as a team. For students who exceeded the objective, the team could qualify for additional incentive pay provided that the 90 percent level was obtained. Chapter 3 details the incentive schedule and the amounts each team received.

The principals of the experimental schools may be thought of as adventurous and willing to try new ways to improve their schools. They are career principals, having served in that capacity for a minimum of fifteen years. They also are stable, mature, and experienced.

Nevertheless, there are differences among these principals and among the members of the four collegial teams. For the purposes of reporting on the collegial team effort, there seems to be little to be gained from any detailed analysis of these differences. The principals, schools, teachers, and students of the schools involved are probably more like other schools in other districts than they are different. The people involved would probably disagree because we all like to think of our schools and their human elements as unique—and they are. Our point here is that their uniqueness does not significantly influence the generalizibility of their responses or of the findings with respect to the collegial team arrangement. It is reasonably safe to predict that their reactions to and with the collegial team scheme was typical of the reactions that could be expected in most American schools. Schools serving students from homes that have a significantly lower socioeconomic base typically face similar problems with only differences in degree of difficulty.

As indicated in earlier chapters, the numbers of students who are more difficult to teach is generally increasing, but the collegial scheme for improving performance in those schools is the same as it is for any other school. Students from lower socioeconomic strata can learn despite the fact that the difficulty in causing that learning to occur is greater. Given that increased difficulty, a collegial team approach is even more defensible as a method for improving outcomes and effectiveness.

The collegial team evaluation model rests upon several assumptions. Some of these assumptions are supported by the writings of others. Attempts to verify other assumptions were made using attitude inventories and questionnaires to determine whether or not the behavior of teachers in a collegial setting reflected those assumptions. Ancedotal records from principals, together with personal interviews, added to the available information on assumption veracity.

Maslow's Hierarchy of Needs

As indicated in Chapter 1, a fundamental point of departure for the collegial team evaluation scheme rests upon Maslow's hierarchy of human needs. The assumption is made that the lower-level survival needs of teachers have been met. According to Maslow, higher-level needs do not emerge until these lower-level needs have been satisfied. Despite the rhetoric that characterizes some of the literature of teacher organizations, teachers do not appear to be fundamentally motivated for action over salaries and fringe benefits. Decision-making involvement is a stronger desire, and that may be taken to imply a need for greater self-determination.

We could theorize then, that teachers are on the threshold of a major breakthrough in the release of creative potential. The school system, if it fails to recognize the need of teachers to become self-actualizing professionals, will retard and repress this need, thus contributing to its own potential for conflict and ineffectiveness. Collegial evaluation procedures provide an environment that encourages the development of creative potential and self-actualization. The responses of both principals and teachers in experimental schools will be seen to have strengthened the behaviors Maslow's theory leads us to expect.

Information Sharing and Team Planning

A second assumption that underpinned the collegial team evaluation scheme was information sharing and team planning. Neither information sharing nor team planning are new or startling assumptions. There is a natural exchange of ideas among teachers that varies with the conduciveness of the environment. Information sharing may be restricted or inhibited in the traditional school setting for several reasons. Among these are (1) lack of encouragement for the activity and a consequent haphazardness. Information is shared sporadically and by change encounter and (2) lack of reward for information sharing. Good teaching techniques may not be shared because an attitude of "why should I" may prevail. Teachers who need help may be isolated by their peers simply because the time and effort required to help them is seen as a burden best left to administrators. Feelings of jealousy, resentment and rejection may plague various members of the teaching staff.

It was assumed that a collegial team setting would promote information sharing by rewarding that kind of behavior in terms of group goals. In addition, specific time for information sharing related to needs expressed by team members was available. Information sharing was legitimized, rewarded and promoted. Team planning was assumed to be related to information sharing. As a concept it is not new, but again, formalizing the process in a collegial team setting promotes such activity. In experimental schools, the responses to a series of questions about information sharing and team planning revealed increased commitment to these behaviors. The assumption that such activity will occur can be converted into a purpose of the team so that it is actively promoted and is rewarding for each member and for the team as a unit.

Interviews with principals concerning team planning and information sharing provided comments from principals and quotes from teachers such as these:

Teachers become more concerned about helping colleagues solve problems.

Teachers are more willing to share ideas and materials.

There is more teamwork among teachers.

We have been able to share our frustrations with our collegial team and felt they were ready to answer any questions we needed answered, with a positive attitude instead of a negative one.

Collegial team idea helped us to see viewpoints of other teachers, therefore I believe we became more understanding. We were able to learn more from each other, certainly helping us with new ideas. There has been a great deal of sharing of ideas.

I believe that the major change is an increased awareness of other levels because of better communications. The support of the entire group has been invaluable during a time of changing teaching patterns and new approaches to curriculum for individualizing. We have drawn strengths and ideas from each other.

I developed a better understanding of and appreciation for the members of the team. Discussing techniques of teaching freely, stimulated new ideas which benefited my attitude and affected the children beneficially.

There were no negative comments with respect to information sharing and team planning, although there were differences in the amount of emphasis on those activities from school to school. Perhaps the same could be said for any random group of schools, however, the degree of the activities does seem to be a function of awareness and promotion in the school.

Task Differentiation

A third assumption in the experimental schools involved the differentiation of tasks. This assumption is based upon the notion that in a collegial team setting, special expertise will be discovered among members and that this expertise will result in task differentiation.

The assumption was confirmed in two schools at a relatively high level. It was not a significant factor in the other two. When presented the opportunity to comment, the teachers offered such statements as the following:

I feel we have developed a better understanding and appreciation of our fellow colleagues on the team. We have the freedom to discuss teaching techniques freely.

Teachers have the opportunity to see their peers practice positive teaching techniques.

Greater respect for fellow teachers has developed.

It may be that the questions used to elicit responses for task differentiation were inadequate. It may be that the teachers involved saw themselves as relatively equal in expertise so that "developing respect" was their way of acknowledging that each of them had a unique contribution to make to the team effort. In any case, there was an obvious emphasis on mutual respect. Identical teacher behavior is neither possible nor desirable, but a process that allows for continual interchange among teachers stimulates growth. A collegial setting promotes the growth of its members.

Personal Relations and Group Solidarity

A fourth assumption was that the collegial team would develop improved personal relations and group solidarity. There was strong evidence from all schools that this assumption was viable. The quotes below express this evidence in a variety of ways:

Our collegial team is a step toward harmonious understanding between teachers. We are more willing to accept each others feelings and attitudes. . . .

Identifying areas of need, sharing ideas, working together creates a positive climate that leads to growth for all concerned.

The collegial team at ———— has emerged as an extremely strong working unit. In the two years it has been in operation, it has grown from individual to a unit approach. . . .

It is, of course, possible that the improvements related to personal relations and group solidarity developed from a "Hawthorne effect." Simply paying attention to the collegial teams may have accounted for much of the observed change as reported by principals and teachers. The fact that these effects persisted for two years suggests that they are positive results with some staying power. In addition, it is easier for the principal to pay attention to a collegial team of teachers than it is for him to divide his time among individuals. This is especially true when the group has jointly developed its objectives and seek common ends.

Team Evaluation

Assumption five, which was anticipated to be the most difficult for teachers to reflect, was based upon the acceptance by teachers of evaluation among themselves. This aspect of the collegial team approach represents the most radical departure from what are considered the "normal" conditions under which teachers perform.

Although results were mixed among the experimental schools, there were positive statements concerning collegial team evaluation from three of the schools. Some quotations related to evaluation follow:

They are constantly re-evaluating methodology, materials and student results. They have gained confidence in themselves and team members to openly question each other.

When teachers observe each other, consult about what is happening in the classroom, and develop evaluations, they become more concerned with each other's successes and failures.

Teachers see the evaluation process as a positive, rather than threatening, activity.

As indicated in Chapter 1, collegial evaluation involves the evaluation of programs, processes, products, and personnel. Personnel evaluation is most sensitive and requires high trust levels before it can be meaningful. The traditional role of the principal changes, and the principal may be more willing to give up that role than teachers are willing to have him give it up. Broadening the range of evaluation data sources and reducing individual threat potential are necessary to help teachers accept collegial team evaluation. Considerable progress in this sensitive area was reported in each experimental school.

Use of Research

Assumption six was based on the notion that a collegial team could make greater use of research findings in the school. Results on this assumption were mixed. Two schools responded positively and two had little to say about the use of research. No particular emphasis was given to this assumption in any of the experimental schools and no reference to it was made in interview sessions. Too great an emphasis on this assumption might well have become a threat to the team, thereby preventing them from achieving growth in other areas. The assumption should not be abandoned, but should receive increasing emphasis as a collegial team matures in mutual trust and group solidarity.

Group Decisions and Problem Solving

That a collegial team will seize upon the opportunity to involve themselves in decision making and problem solving was the essence of assumption seven and is, of course, related directly to assumption one. The experimental schools were very positive in their reactions on this assumption. It is a highly professional activity and supports the literature on participative management. The notion that teachers want to be professional rather than seeing themselves as mere "labor" is also supported. The following quotations from interviews and questionnaires are offered in substantiation:

Teachers feel more involved in administrative decisions because they are consulted about all matters which involve the team.

There is less fear of the administration.

Collegial team shared decision making is based on mutual trust and faith; that fact alone opens the avenues for improved performance among team members and leads to a variety of options to solve identified problems.

In my opinion, the total school climate changed as the team became more and more involved in an open, shared decision-making format.

Involving team members in the interviewing and selection of prospective team members is a major plus factor.

Participative management, widely advocated in the literature, and the subject of much educational rhetoric, can be meaningfully achieved in the collegial team schema. Participative management does not mean the abandonment of leadership by the principal, but is instead a communications process that opens the decision-making act to broadbased input. The role changes required of a school principal in participative management are essentially the same as the role changes required for successful collegial team evaluation.

The final quotation above suggests a technique that was widely used in the experimental schools. Selecting teachers has traditionally been a central office or administrative function. In a collegial team, the principal, relinquishing some of his traditional decision-making prerogative, involves the collegial team in selecting replacements and paraprofessional aides. This one act on the part of the principal speaks volumes about his commitment to the collegial team concept. The team interviews prospective candidates, and together with the principal, they decide which candidates are most likely to have the kind of expertise and compatibility that will improve the effectiveness of the team. In larger school districts, where the central personnel office has often exclusively selected teachers, principals should insist that collegial teams at least have the opportunity to interview from a list of candidates. Teachers should no longer be arbitrarily assigned to schools, except in those cases where declining enrollment forces the district to reassign surplus teachers.

The experimental schools reacted to collegial team involvement in staff selection with comments such as these:

Involving team members in the interviewing and selection of prospective team members is a major plus factor.

Our collegial team was more than willing to come together during the summer to interview teacher candidates. We interviewed six prospects and the teacher we selected will, we feel, strengthen our team in several ways. In addition, we feel some responsibility to make sure he is successful and pleased to work with us.

Changing Role of the Principal

Few changes of any importance or significance can occur in a school without the active support of the principal. Lipham and Hoeh (1975) indicate that changing adult behavior is a prerequisite to attaining all other objectives. The principal must devote a great deal of time to the development of staff capability in problem solving, decision making, and personal relations with adults and children. Operationally, the administration of a school inevitably performs within a network of person-to-person interaction.

Many authors lament the "caught-in-the-middle" role of the principal. His power is reduced. He is subject to pressure from the central office, the teacher organization, a variety of communities, and his own personal need disposition. Despite all these negative analyses, there is evidence that principals remain in place for extended periods of time and that they do not frequently opt out of the position voluntarily.

It is generally accepted that the principal is the instructional leader in his school and that he is ultimately responsible for its operation. Via the accountability process, the responsibility of the principal is defined through goals. The goals are usually districtwide in nature and become imposed upon schools even though the school may itself be involved in goal setting. Responsibility to attain objectives related to those goals is also imposed. The principal has a choice in *how* he will direct the attainment of objectives in an accountability system, but no choice in whether or not he *will* direct efforts to those ends.

The collegial team schema provides a means for the principal to carry out his responsibility to direct the attainment of objectives within a system of accountability. He shares power (knowledge) with his collegial teams and imposes responsibility for results. In the process, he encourages teachers to believe in their ability to perform and produce as a team. By reversing the traditional labor-management approach, he builds a professional commitment to meeting the learning needs of students. Experimental results with collegial team schools confirm that both teachers and principals are willing and able to build that kind of relationship.

The quotations below illustrate the reactions of experimental school principals to the collegial team concept:

The collegial team concept at this school has done more to change teacher-principal-support staff behavior than any other effort to improve climate for learning.

My role as principal has really changed. I have become a questioner. I try to ask my questions in ways that do not create negative anxieties, but lead to a variety of options to solve identified problems.

The collegial team concept, in my opinion, has been the most exciting step we have ever taken toward improving professional cooperation among teachers. The collegial team concept takes time to develop and mature. Each of us had to learn to give and take—including the principal who had always been the decisionmaker.

It should be clear that these principals volunteered to participate in the experiment so that positive reactions could be expected. Their enthusiasm was, nevertheless, genuine and could be traced to a sense of accomplishment, together with better staff relationships, greater cooperation and productivity, and higher levels of professionalism throughout the school.

Curriculum Articulation and Integration

In any discussion of the curriculum for schools, articulation and integration are generally considered as prime ingredients. Articulation means that the curriculum has continuity and sequence over time. A classic example is the program in reading at the elementary level. Children do not learn to read in grade one, nor grade two, nor grade three. The objective is to produce independent readers by the end of grade three. If the reading program is not articulated over time, the objective will be missed with large numbers of children. It is not uncommon to find fully half of the children in an elementary school reading one or more grade level equivalents below their expectancy. Unless remediated, this condition is cumulative so that the children involved fall further and further behind as they progress through the school.

If a curriculum program is to have continuity and sequence over time, then some method of controlling what happens to children in classrooms must be found. Control in this context has serious implications. It suggests several conditions that may be difficult to produce in an elementary school with the current emphasis on decentralization, democratic administration, participative management, and individualization of instruction, an emphasis which is often misplaced, misunderstood, or misinterpreted. Among these conditions are the following:

1. First grade teachers must know the skills students learn in preschool or kindergarten classes. Second level teachers must know the skills students learn in first grade and so forth up the line.
2. A record of the progress of each child must be established and forwarded with him to each successive level.
3. The use of materials must be monitored so that an agreed upon sequence can be maintained.
4. Unlearned skills must be diagnosed and retaught in a variety of ways until they are mastered.
5. Individual teacher entreprenuring must be monitored so that an agreed-upon skill sequence is not violated. Children who are difficult to teach do not respond well to a program that changes drastically from level to level in its approach and skill-building sequence.
6. Student progress must be monitored frequently so that reteaching decisions can be made before the student falls hopelessly behind. Too many students are condemned to failure in the early grades—a condition which is self-defeating for the child and difficult for a school to correct.
7. The curriculum to be implemented must be selected or developed by the teachers who are expected to use it. Many curriculum materials are available, in fact, the array is often bewildering.

Whether or not a given set is successful in helping students learn is often, if not always, a function of teacher commitment. If teachers believe in a program, they can make it produce results. Knowing a program and being committed to it means the teachers understand the weaknesses that are inherent in any program and can do what is necessary to plug the holes and make it work. There probably is no program that works with every child. Plugging the holes in a basic program that works with most students makes it possible to deal effectively with students who do not respond to that program so that the success ratio should be 90 percent.

The conditions just described are possible if a program is implemented by a collegial team. All the assumptions explored earlier in this chapter reinforce the articulation of the curriculum and they are viable in a collegial team setting. Control then rests with a team of professionals lead by the principal. The alternative is a set of individuals who introduce so many variables in approach, sequence, vocabulary, and beliefs that articulation is impossible. Such a condition is very democratic for teachers but disastrous for large numbers of students. Students do not learn to read in one teacher's classroom. They learn to read over time. Obviously, the task for teachers and students is made easier if there is an agreed-upon articulated program that has scope and sequence over time.

An integrated curriculum is one that is interdisciplinary in character. The skills learned in one area of the curriculum reinforce skills acquired in another. A collegial team of teachers can integrate the curriculum because they are constantly interacting as they plan, monitor and evaluate programs, processes, and products. A review of the quotations from collegial teams provided earlier in this chapter will confirm that attention to curriculum integration becomes a natural activity when a professional team learns to work together.

The reader may have wondered why, in the experimental schools, the success figure was set such that 90 percent of the students had to reach the target growth of one grade level equivalent in reading before the collegial team was eligible for the bonus or supplementary plan. The reason should now be clear. The experimentors believe that a collegial team of professionals can produce that kind of a result. In effect, the 90 percent target becomes an expectation for the collegial team. It represents a success ratio with students that is both desirable and possible, but rarely attained in any school. The experimental collegial teams did not reject that target. If they thought it was unreasonable, they did not make that fact known to their principals, or the experimentors. Can we infer that they also believe that 90 out of every 100 students can gain one grade equivalent in reading every year? School policymakers should set such targets. High expectations produce high achievement. Diluted processes of accountability can be expected to produce diluted results. Parents and school boards expect more. Superintendents and principals desire more. Collegial teams of professionals can produce more, and they know they can. In the process, their ego status and self-actualization needs are satisfied. For students, success in reading is related to a healthy self-image and to feelings of adequacy and success with the total school experience.

Summary

Attitude scales, personal interviews, and anecdotal records provided by experimental school principals were used to examine the personal reactions of experimental school teachers and principals to the collegial team schema. These reactions, as evidenced by the quotations shown above and from attitude response analysis confirmed the veracity of many of the assumptions that underlie the collegial team concept. Perhaps the most important of these assumptions is the one that appeals to teachers' need to be professional. Professionalism can be linked directly to the higher order belonging needs, ego-status needs, and the need for self-actualization espoused by Maslow. The basic needs and safety needs of teachers have been met. The school, as a system, must provide mechanisms for meeting these higher order needs. Currently, they generaly do not. Actually, because the system is unresponsive to these needs, it is pushing itself toward a more repressive and less responsive mode characterized by rigid labor-management structures. It is difficult to see how any of the current collective bargaining models will do anything to release human potential. Furthermore, there is evidence that teachers basically resent the movement toward collective bargaining and would prefer a more professional role with loyalty to the public power structure of which they are a significant part.

The collegial team experimental results, when combined with the personal responses of the professionals involved, support the notion that collegial teams are a significant departure from the traditional school system mode of operation and offer teachers and principals an acceptable and professional means for achieving the higher order needs to which they aspire.

The collegial team interval shift analysis scheme was designed to positively address several major issues in education in the 1970s. These issues are interrelated but may be defined as problems of teacher evaluation, problems associated with enrollment decline, and problems of teacher militancy.

The collegial team schema provides a method of changing the current labor-management model used in the evaluation of teachers to a model that places professional responsibility in the hands of professional groups of teachers. It is contended that teachers want the kind of professional responsibility that preserves their intuitive loyalty to the public power structure and at the same time entrusts them with the evaluation of accountability for themselves, their processes, their programs, and their products. Professionalism for teachers will remain a myth until this responsibility is given to and accepted by teachers.

The interval shift analysis plan provides an institutional profit-sharing or incentive system that addresses problems brought on by enrollment decline. Students who find learning difficult have always been present in schools. As their numbers increase, it is even more imperative that the schools find more effective ways to cause learning to occur. The prime ingredient is the teacher. An incentive system that rewards teachers differentially in favor of students who find it most difficult to succeed is long overdue. Individual merit pay schemes are divisive, administratively unmanageable, and generally unacceptable to teachers. The interval shift incentive plan rewards group excellence and enhances teachers' desires to behave as true professionals. It holds promise for reuniting the instructional delivery system of schools through cooperative team effort among teachers, principals, and resource people.

In the process, teacher militance can be effectively reduced because the system will provide more adequately for the ego-status and self-actualization needs of the people involved. Boards of education and the public they represent might well renew their faith in the public schools they support and be more willing to increase that support if they saw a system that was more professional in terms of self-accountability.

School administrators, currently uncomfortably in the middle between a discontented public owner and a militant employee organization, should embrace a system that brings professionals back together as a team. A divided system is vulnerable to legislative whim and caprice. Teacher groups and administrator groups locked in an internal power struggle invite lack of support.

The public schools can be better than they are. They can be more responsive to student needs. They can elicit greater public support. They can be more professional. The collegial team interval shift analysis concept moves schools toward those ends.

Appendixes

Appendix A
Computer Program for Net Shift Analysis

Use of Net Shift Analysis Program

Card 1   Variable Format Card for input data

I.D. of School Site   either   4A1   or   4A4
Grade Level of Student   I2
Pre test Score   F3.1
Post test Score   F3.1
    (4A1, 12X, 2 F3.1)

Card 2   Variable Format Card to set Parameters for Model

1. Minimum Gain Required
2. Percentage of Goal which must be met in order to qualify for additional funding
3. Additional Bonus for gains greater than the goal on Supplementary Plan
4. Total regular bonus if goal is met
5. Incentive payment for reaching 50% of the goal

Card 3   Output Format for Analysis

School I.D. 4A1 or 4A4 (Same as used in Card 1)
Pre test Score
Post test Score
Grade Level
    (1X, 4A1, 12X, F3.1, 10X, F3.1, 10X, 13)

Card 4   Parameters for the Incentive Model as specified in Format Card 2

Card 5 ⎫
        ⎬   School Site input data according to format specified in Card 1
Card $n + 5$ ⎭

****   end of file test for first School Site

        ⎫
        ⎬   repeat as many times as required for each school site analysis
        ⎭

****
/* ——— end of file test for entire analysis

```
FORTRAN IV G LEVEL  21                    MAIN                    DATE = 75314           11/14/33

0001              DIMENSION X(200,6),CIF(200),GRA(10,4),CIF(2000),GRA(10,4),TEA(10,4),
1SCH(50,4),FM(20),FM2(20),FM2(20)
0002              DIMENSION FM3(20)
0003              DIMENSION FM3(20)
0004              DIMENSION IGF(2000)
0005              DIMENSION SUM1(20),SUM2(20),ICT(20),ICT(20),AV1(20),AV2(20)
0006              DATA STR/1H*/
0007              READ(5,1)(FA(J),J=1,20)
0008              READ(5,1)(FM2(J),J=1,20)
0009    1         FORMAT(20A4)
0010              READ(5,1)(FM3(J),J=1,20)
0011              WRITE(5,FM2)XCCDE,XPCT,FACT,TCF,XNED,XDAY
0012    8743      FORMAT(FN(J),J=1,20)
0013              WRITE(2X,*THE DATA INPUT FORMAT=*,20A4)
0014    100       FORMAT(6,1CD)XCCDE,TARGET,CE,FOR EACH STUDENT=*,F34.2/5X,*MINIMUM PC
1CF EACH ADDITICNAL GE, GROWTH=*,F17.2/5X,*ADDITICNAL BCNUS
1VING 1CCX CF GCAL=*,F23.2/5X,*INCENTIVE FCR ACHIE
1*,F31.5/5X,*MAXIMUM ALLOWABLE CAYS OF SCHOOL MISSED=*,F24.2)
0015              N=6
0016    974       WRITE(M,974)
0017              FORMAT(10X,10HPERCENTAGE,5X,5HTCTAL,4X,6HMIDDLE,5X,5HBCNUS)
0018              XMIC=C
0019              DC 695
0020    695       WRITE(6,2525)I=1,10
0021    2525      FCRMAT(1F0)
0022              FCT=C
0023              XMIC=XMIC*100
0024              DO 695  I=1,25
0025              PCT=PCT+*C4
0026              CALL XF(FCT,TCF,XMIC,SALE,XX)
0027              WRITE(6,433)PCT,TCF,XMIC,SALE,XX
0028    433       FORMAT(10X,F15.2)
0029              CCNTINUE
0030    559       CCNTINUE
0031              WRITE(6,5C2)
0032    5C2       FORMAT(5X,*STUDENTS IN THE PLAN*)
0033              WRITE(6,2525)
0034              NV1=6
0035              II=6
0036              I2=5
0037    2926      WRITE(6,2926)
                  FCRMAT(10X,*THESE ARE THE STUDENTS INCLUDING THOSE WITH MISSIN
0038    1G CATA*)
0039              DC 2958  KLJM=1,10
0040              DO 8C5  J=1,12
0041              IIC(J)=C
0042              SUM1(J)=C
0043              SUM2(J)=C
0044              AV1(J)=C
0045    8C9       AV2(J)=0
0046              CCNTINUE
0047              ITCT=0
0048              X7=0
                  XCUT=2.5
```

```
FORTRAN IV G LEVEL  21                    MAIN                  DATE = 75314        11/14/33        PAGE CCC2

0C49            X1=0
0050            AC=0
0C51            AK=0
0C52            JJDDR=0
0C53            DC 40  I=1,10CC
0C54     562    REAC(5,FM,END=219)(X(I,J),(X(I,J),J=1,4),IGF(I),(X(I,J),J=5,6)
0C55            IF(X(I,1).EC. STF)   GC TC 29S
0C56            ITCT=ITCT+1
0C57            IF(X(I,1) .EQ. STAR)   GC TC 29S
0C58            IF(X(I,1) .EC. STF)   GC TC 299
0C59            IF(IGR(I) .NE. 1) XCCCE=1.0
0C60            IX11=IGR(I)
0C61            IF(IX11.GT.12)  GC TC 802
0C62            ISUM1(IX11)=SLM1(IX11)+X(I,5)
0C63            SUM2(IX11)=SLM2(IX11)+X(I,6)
0C64     8C2    IICT(IX11)=IICT(IX11)+1
0C65            DIF(I)=X(I,I1)-X(I,I2)
0C66            IF(X(I,I1) .EQ. 0) X(I,I1)=1.0
0C67            IF(X(I,I2) .EQ. C) X(I,12)=1
0C68     8C2    IF(CIF(I) .CE. XCCDE)  AC=NC+1
0C69            AK=AK+1
0C70            X7=X7+DIF(I)
0C71            X1=X1+DIF(I)(1)-XCCCE)
0C72     40     CCNTINUE
0C73            CCNTINUE
0C74     40     CCNTINUE
0C75     39S    CCNTINUE
0C76     29S    CCNTINUE
0C77            WRITE(6,2920)  ITCT
0C78     2920   FCRMAT(1CX,'THE TCTAL NLMBER OF STLDENTS=',110)
0C79            CD= X(I,I1)-X(I,I2)
0C80            WRITE(6,2525)
0C81            WRITE(6,2925)
0C82     2925   FORMAT(10X,'THESE ARE THE STUDENTS FCR WHICH WE HAVE CCMPLETE
0C83            1CATA')
0C84            DC 31  I=1,AK
0C85            CDD=X(I,I1)-X(I,I2)
0C86            WRITE(6,FM3)(X(I,J),J=1,NV1),IGR(I)
0C87     31     CCNTINUE
0C88            FACT=25.00
0C89            WRITE(6,2521)  AK
0C90     2921   FORMAT(1CX,'TOTAL NLMBER OF STUDENTS WITH CCMFLETE CATA',11C)
0C91            DC 61C IKW=1,12
0C92            IX11=IICT(IKW)
0C93            IF(IX11 .EC. C)  GC TC 61C
0C94            AV1(IKW)=SLM1(IKW)/>11
0C95            AV2(IKW)=SLM2(IKW)/>11
0C96     61C    CCNTINUE
0C97            WRITE(6,3003)
0C98     3003   1 FCST,2X,'AVERAGE PRE',2X,'NUMBER OF STUDENTS',2X,'SUM PRE',2X,'SUM
                  FCRMAT(2X,'GRACE',2X,'AVERAGE PRE',2X,'AVERAGE FCST')
0C9C            DC 3001  IKW=1,12
C100            IF(AV1(IKW) .EC. C)  GC TC 3CC1
```

```
0101            WRITE(6,3002) IKM,IICT(IKM),SLM1(IKM),SLM2(IKM),AV1(IKM),AV2(IKM)
0102   3002     FORMAT(I7,2X,I18,2X,F7.2,2X,F6.2,2X,F12.2,F12.2)
0103   3001     CONTINUE
0104            X2=NK
0105            X3=NC
0106            FCT=X3/X2
0107            IJERK=0
0108            XPCT=.75
0109   7745     CONTINUE
0110            IF(PCT .LT. XPCT)      GC TC 45
0111            FAY1=FACT*X7
0112            CALL XP(FCT,TCF,XMEC,SALE,XX)
0113            FAY2=SALE
0114            TPAY=PAY1+PAY2
0115            GO TC 50
0116   45       CONTINUE
0117            FAY1=0
0118            CALL XP(FCT,TCF,XMEC,SALE,XX)
0119            FAY2=SALE
0120            TFAY=PAY1+FAY2
0121   50       WRITE(6,520) FAY1,FAY2,TPAY
0122   520      FORMAT(5X,'SUPPLEMENTARY INCENTIVE FAAN FAYMENT=',F10.2/5X,'REC
0123           1ULAT INCENTIVE PLAN PAYMENT=',F16.2/5X,'TCTAL INCENTIVE PLAN FAYME
0124           1NT=',F16.2)
0125            WRITE(6,541) XX
0126   541      FORMAT(5X,'THE EXPENDT FCR THE FUNCTICN=',F17.2)
0127            X4=X7
0128            WRITE(6,2315) X4
0129   2315     FORMAT(5X,'CUMULATIVE G.E. ABCVE CCAL',F21.2)
0130            WRITE(6,2358) FCT
0131   2358     FORMAT(5X,'FCT ABCVE CCAL=',F33.3)
0132            WRITE(6,2983) XPCT
0133   2983     FORMAT(5X,'MINIMUM FCT TO CLALIFY FCR SLFFLEMENTARY=',F7.3)
0134            WRITE(6,2525)
0135            IDCRK=0
0136            IDCRK=1
0137            IF(IDCRK .EC. 0) GC TC 7741
0138            IJERK=IJERK .EQ. 5) GC TC 7741
0139            IJERK=IJERK+1
0140            XCCN=.05
0141            XPCT=XPCT-XCCN
0142            WRITE(6,2525)
0143            GO TC 7745
0144   7741     CONTINUE
0145            X4=0
0146            NTC=0
0147            WRITE(6,2924)
0148   2924     FORMAT(10X,'THESE ARE THE STUCENTS WHO CAINEC AT LEAST 1 G.E.
0149           1GROWTH OR HIGHER.')
0150            WRITE(6,3322)
        3322     FORMAT(5X,'STUDENT NAME',2X,'PRE AND PCST TEST SCORES',2X,'CIFF
               1ERENCE',2X,'ANT AECVE CCAL')
                DO 2314    I=1,NK
```

```
0151            DIF(I)=X(I,I1)-X(I,I2)
0152            IF(IGR(I).EG.1)XCCDE=.8
0153            IF(IGR(I).NE.1)XCCDE=1.0
0154            IF(DIF(I).LT.XCCDE) GC TC 2314
0155            DD=DIF(I)-XCCDE
0156            X4=X4+DD
0157            NTOT=NTOT+1
0158            WRITE(6,20)(X(I,J),J=1,NV1),DIF(I),DD,IGR(I)
0159         20 FCRMAT(2X,4A4,4F10.2,I10)
0160       2314 CCNTINUE
0161            WRITE(6,2922)  NTOT
0162       2922 FCRMAT(10X,'THE TOTAL NUMBER CF STUDENTS REACHING 1 G.E. CFCWT
             1H=',I10)
0163            X11=0
0164            X12=0
0165            DO 5414    I=1,NK
0166            IF(IGR(I).EG.1) XCCDE=.8
0167            IF(IGR(I).NE.1) XCCDE=1.0
0168            IF(DIF(I).LT.C)  GC TC 5412
0169            X12=X12+DIF(I)-XCCDE
0170            GC TO 5414
0171       5412 CCNTINUE
0172            X11=X11+DIF(I)-XCCDE
0173       5414 CCNTINUE
0174            WRITE(6,2199)  X12,X11
0175       2199 FCRMAT(5X,'CUMULATIVE C.E. ABCVE GCAL=',F10.2/5X,'CUMULATIVE G
             1E. BELCW GCAL=',F1C.2)
0176       2998 CCNTINUE
0177        219 CCNTINUE
0178            STOP
0179            END
```

```
FORTRAN IV G LEVEL  21                    MAIN                    DATE = 75314                    11/14/73                    PAGE 0002

*OPTIONS IN EFFECT*  ID,EBCDIC,SOURCE,NOLIST,NODECK,LOAD,NOMAP
*OPTIONS IN EFFECT*  NAME=MAIN    , LINECNT=56
*STATISTICS*  SOURCE STATEMENTS = , PROGRAM SIZE =      71190
*STATISTICS*  NO DIAGNOSTICS GENERATED

=============================== P A G E   S K I P   S U P P R E S S E D ===============================

FORTRAN IV G LEVEL  21                    XP                     DATE = 75314                    11/14/73                    PAGE 0001

0001              SUBROUTINE XP(PCT,TOF,XMID,SALE,XX)
0002              XPCT=PCT
0003        223   IF(TOP) 221,221,223
0004        224   IF(XMID) 221,221,224
0005              CONTINUE
0006              IF(PCT) 21,22,22
0007         21   CONTINUE
0008        221   SALE=0
0009              GO TO 24
0010         22   CONTINUE
0011              PCT=.5
0012              XX=(ALOG10(XMID)-ALOG10(TOF))/ALOG10(PCT)
0013         10   IF(XX) 10,11,10
0014              CONTINUE
0015              PCT=XPCT
0016              SALE=TOF*FCT**XX
0017              GO TO 24
0018         11   CONTINUE
0019              SALE=TOP
0020         24   CONTINUE
0021              RETURN
0022              END
0023
```

Appendix B
Survey of Teacher Attitudes

Note: Respondents were asked to scale-rate the questionnaire items below as follows: 1 = Strongly Agree; 2 = Agree; 3 = No Opinion; 4 = Disagree; and 5 = Strongly Disagree. They were also instructed to rate items 1-21 on the basis of their perceptions of schools in general and items 22-39, according to their own particular schools.

1. If teachers are involved in curriculum decision making, they are less likely to be involved in activities that might lead to sanctions or lockouts.
2. Having teachers involved in curriculum decision making would result in higher cognitive growth for students.
3. Teacher evaluation of each other is an excellent mechanism for increasing overall teaching performance.
4. A strategy for increasing the professionalism of teachers would be to have teachers involved in all aspects of curricular decisions.
5. For increasing professionalism among teachers, it is important that teachers are involved in the evaluation of each other rather than leaving evaluation strictly to administrators.
6. Some students are "left out" in the classroom because they require an inordinate amount of attention from the teacher.
7. If a teacher is to be evaluated on classroom performance, it is better for teachers to work with the good and average students and to spend less time and effort struggling with the slower students.
8. Some students do not receive their fair share of instructional resources from the teacher.
9. By and large central office support services, curriculum specialists, etc., are a waste of money in terms of boosting teaching performance at a school.
10. There are teachers who could and should be helped in terms of improving their teaching performance but they are neglected because there is no incentive.
11. Only fellow teachers can help improve the teaching performance of other teachers.

12. It would be nice if educators had some way of financially rewarding the better teachers.

13. In terms of teacher support, it would be better to have a "group" profit-sharing plan for an entire school rather than have individual merit pay for teachers.

14. The primary reason teachers consider striking is monetary.

15. The primary reason teachers consider striking is because the conditions of learning and the conditions under which a teacher is evaluated are poor.

16. Student learning is better served when teams of teachers are involved together in instruction and evaluation.

17. Teachers are happiest and most content when they are treated as professionals when it comes to evaluation and decision making.

18. If school administrators could get away with it, they would probably increase the work load of teachers.

19. Probationary teachers should be granted tenure only upon the recommendation of the permanent teachers.

20. A teacher should practice his ideas on what is best for students even though the administration prefers other methods.

21. To do his best, a teacher needs to know what is going on in the whole school.

22. Teachers are heavily involved in curriculum decision making.

23. Teachers evaluate other teachers for the purpose of improving teaching performance.

24. Teachers at our school are less militant than those at other schools.

25. Some students, because they are slower, do not get the attention they need.

26. Slower students get commensurately more teacher attention than fast students.

27. There is no need for teachers to give advice to other teachers for improving teaching performance because all are equally competent.

28. There is a serious teacher morale problem since teachers do not have a voice in decision making.

29. Teachers at our school are unhappy with the school district

more for reasons centered around the instructional system than for more money.

30. Teachers often use the instructional resources of the school district such as curriculum specialists, media centers and other central office services.

31. The administrators interfere with what teachers know is the best way to teach children.

32. Teachers are left alone to make all decisions related to instruction.

33. Permanent teachers are heavily involved in the hiring of new staff and granting of tenure.

34. The administrator consults teachers on class scheduling, teacher assignments, transfer plans, discipline, promotion, and instructional loads.

35. Teachers are in constant communication with each other and know what other teachers are doing.

36. Teachers know who the poor performing teachers are.

37. Every effort is made to assist poor performing teachers.

38. Teachers are centrally involved in making major educational policy decisions.

39. Teachers who stick their necks out by taking a definite policy position are looked down upon by administrators.

References

References

Action, 1975, Calif. Teachers Association, Vol. 13, No. 13 Burlingame, California, April 11, 1975.

Anderson, Lester W. 1970. "Management Team Versus Collective Bargaining for Principals." *NASSP Bulletin* (May): 169-76.

Bruno, James E. 1970. *How to Use Modern Management Techniques in Decision Making*. Swarthmore, Pa.: A.C. Croft.

_____. 1972a. "Interval Shift Analysis." *American Education Research Journal* (Spring): 175-195.

_____. ed. 1972b. *Emerging Issues in Education*. Lexington, Mass.: Lexington Books, D.C. Heath and Co.

Derr, C. Brooklyn and John J. Gabarro. 1972. "An Organizational Contingency Theory for Education. *Educational Administration Quarterly* VII, no. 2 (Spring): 26.

Drucker, Peter F. 1968. *The Age of Discontinuity* New York: Harper and Row.

English, Fenwick and James Zaharis. 1972. "Crisis in Middle Management," *NASSP Bulletin* (April): 1-9.

Filogamo, Martin J. 1970. "New Angle on Accountability." *Today's Education* 59 (May): 53.

Fox, James. 1970. "Issues in Performance Contracting." Working Paper, Urban Educational Policy and Planning, University of California, Los Angeles.

Glasman, N.S., Lillait, B.R., and Gmelch W. 1974. *Evaluation of Instructors in Higher Education: Concepts, Research and Development*. Regents of the University of California, Los Angeles, pp. 1-6.

Hall, George R. 1970. "Issues in Performance Contraction for Educational Services." Document WN-7144-HEW, Rand Corporation, Santa Monica, Calif.

Hall, George R., and Stucker, J.P., "The Performance Contracting Concept in Education" RAND Corp., R-6991. HEW, May, 1971.

Herrick, Mary J. 1962. *Merit Rating: Dangerous Mirage or Master Plan*. American Federation of Teachers, New York, p. 64.

_____. 1962. *Merit Rating—Won't Solve Problems of Public Education*. American Federation of Teachers, New York, p. 13.

Lessinger, Leon M. 1970. "Accountability in Public Education." *Today's Education* 59 (May): 52-53.

Likert, Rensis. 1967. *The Human Organization*, New York: Mc-Graw Hill, Inc.

Lindman, Erick. 1970. *New Shift Analysis for Comparing Raw Score Distributions*. Working Paper No. 8, Center for the Study of Evaluation, UCLA, Los Angeles, Cal.

Lipham, James M. and James A. Hoeh. 1974. *The Principalship: Foundations and Functions*. New York: Harper and Row.

Lortie, Dan C. 1971. "Structure and Teacher Performance: A Prologue to Systematic Research." *How Teachers Make a Difference*. Washington, D.C.: U.S. Department of HEW, p. 52.

Maslow, Abraham. 1970. *Motivation and Personality*, 2nd. ed. New York: Harper and Row.

McGregor, Douglas. 1957. "The Human Side of Enterprise." *The Management Review* 46, no. 11, pp. 22-29. © 1957 by the American Management Association, Inc.

Miller, R.I. 1972. *Evaluating Faculty Performance*. San Francisco: Jossey-Bass.

Mood, Alexander. 1971. *How Teachers Make a Difference*. Washington, D.C.: U.S. Government Printing Office, pp. 1 and 2.

North Carolina State Department of Public Instruction. 1965. The *North Carolina Teacher Merit Pay Study*. Durham, N.C., p. 116.

Nottingham, M.A. and Clint Taylor. 1973. Promoting Collegial Efforts in Schools. Norwalk-La Mirada document. Norwalk-La Mirada Unified School District, Norwalk, Calif.

Oklahoma Legislature. 1969. *Education Summary*. Oklahoma City, p. 116.

Silberman, Charles E., 1970. *Crisis In The Classroom*, N.Y. Random House.

"Total Performance Package Dispute Still Unresolved." 1970. *Nation's Schools* 86 (September): 32.

Tucker, J.P. and G.R. Hall. 1971. "The Performance Contracting Concept in Education." Document R-6991-HEW, Rand Corporation, Santa Monica, Calif.

Index

Index

About the Authors

James E. Bruno is Associate Professor at the University of Southern California at Los Angeles teaching in the area of quantitative methods for educational policy and planning. He is consultant to the RAND Corporation and numerous state and local education agencies. He is the author of the two books *Emerging Issues in Education Policy Implications for the Schools*, (Lexington Books, D.C. Heath and Co.) and *Educational Policy Analysis: A quantitative approach*, (Crane Russak) and over thirty publications in the area of educational policy analysis.

Marvin A. Nottingham is Assistant Professor of School Administration in the School of Education at the University of Southern California. He served twenty-three years in the public schools as a teacher, principal, and assistant superintendent. He is consultant to school districts on management accountability, and declining enrollment and has authored a variety of publications in these areas.

Related Lexington Books

Conant, Eaton, H., *Teacher and Paraprofessional Work Productivity*, 224 pp., 1973

Doyle, Kenneth O., *Student Evaluation of Teacher Instruction*, 192 pp., 1975.